Northrop Frye (1912–1991) was one of the most celebrated literary scholars of the twentieth century, and a distinguished professor at the University of Toronto for over fifty years. Among his many books and articles are *The Anatomy of Criticism, Fearful Symmetry, The Educated Imagination, The Great Code: The Bible and Literature,* and *Words with Power.*

The publication of *The Great Code* in 1982 and that of *Words with Power* in 1990 were literary events of major significance. In these two books Frye took what he called 'a fresh and firsthand look' at the Bible and analysed it as a literary critic, exploring its relation to Western literature and its impact on the creative imagination. He described *The Double Vision* as 'something of a shorter and more accessible version' of *The Great Code* and its sequel, *Words with Power.* In simpler context and briefer compass, it elucidates and expands on the ideas and concepts introduced in those books.

The Double Vision is Northrop Frye's last work. It reflects the passions that informed his life – literature, myth, the creative imagination – and the skill with which he communicated those passions to students and readers around the world.

Northrop Frye

The Double Vision

Language and Meaning in Religion

UNIVERSITY
OF
TORONTO PRESS

Toronto Buffalo London

© University of Toronto Press 1991
Toronto   Buffalo   London
Printed in Canada

ISBN 0-8020-5925-2 (cloth)
ISBN 0-8020-6865-0 (paper)

∞

Printed on acid-free paper

Canadian Cataloguing in Publication Data

Frye, Northrop, 1912–91
The double vision: language and meaning in religion
Includes bibliographical references.
ISBN 0-8020-5925-2 (bound)   ISBN 0-8020-6865-0 (pbk.)
1. Bible and literature. 2. Religion and culture.
3. Languages – Religious aspects. I. Title.
PN56.B5F7 1991a   809'.93522   C91-093101-1

for Elizabeth

For double the vision my eyes do see,
And a double vision is always with me:
With my inward eye 'tis an old man grey;
With my outward a thistle across my way.

William Blake

Contents

Northrop Frye: An Appreciation
by Johan Aitken
xi

Preface
xvii

1 The Double Vision of Language
3

The Whirligig of Time, 1925–90
3
Primitive and Mature Societies
7
The Crisis in Language
14

2 The Double Vision of Nature
22

Natural and Human Societies
22
Criticism and Civilization
28

The Redemption of Nature
34

3 The Double Vision of Time
40

Space and Time
40
Time and History
46
Time and Education
52

4 The Double Vision of God
59

Gods and God
59
Hebraic and Hellenic Traditions
65
Metaphorical Literalism
69
The Humanized God
74

Notes
87

Northrop Frye: An Appreciation

The Double Vision is Northrop Frye's last published work and, in many ways, his most accessible. For those who come fresh to this original thinker, there could be no more splendid introduction than these four brief chapters. For those readers worldwide who are steeped in his teachings, this slim volume is a rare distillation of the author's works.

In this text, Frye synthesizes and highlights the major themes of his life's work. There is a compression here that somehow still encompasses the insights of the brief, bright hour (spread throughout his life), which Frye describes as the inspiration for the rest of it. The beautifully turned phrase and the familiar wit are ever present and ever new. He speaks of that 'celebrated ceramic,' for example, in reference to the Grecian urn of Keats' poem. He talks about the perverted myth of erotic love and commitment reduced in our time to 'rutting in rubber.' Frye has observed repeatedly that he repeats himself and that he wouldn't trust any writer who did not. He adds that what he hopes for, of course, is an increase in lucidity. And, in lucidity, nothing he has written surpasses *The Double Vision*.

In these pages, not only are all the times of Northrop Frye eternally present; there are intimations and echoes of his earlier books as well. *Fearful Symmetry*, for example, in which we first meet William Blake's notion of the double vision, is at the heart of the matter; for beyond all poets, Frye seeks recourse to Blake. The four mythoi of literature described in *The Anatomy of Criticism* –

comedy, romance, irony, and tragedy – are mentioned explicitly and taken for granted throughout. We realize that however much we may balk against categories, we would be inarticulate, and our ability to talk about the language of literature mangled and muzzled, without the language of criticism Frye gave to his students and, through the *Anatomy*, gave to the world. The symbolism of apocalyptic and demonic imagery, genuine mythology and its perverted forms, and the primacy of poetry are interwoven for us here. In spite of the resonances from many individual books, the two which form the backdrop to *The Double Vision* are *The Great Code* and *Words with Power*. Together they constitute the 'big book about the Bible' that his friend and colleague Barker Fairley long ago urged him to write. For the reader, *The Double Vision* may serve equally well as either a prologue or an epilogue to those more massive texts.

In a legendary undergraduate course, Frye reminded his students that when the Bible is historically accurate, it is only accidentally so: reporting was not of the slightest interest to its writers. They had a story to tell which could only be told by myth and metaphor: what they wrote became a source of vision rather than doctrine. For the reader, the *historical event* is now 'out of our range' – only the *verbal event* concerns us. While acknowledging the literary qualities of the Bible – what Blake called the 'great code of art' – Frye considers that it would be absurd to see the Bible as only a work of literature. What we need to recognize is that it is written in the language of literature – the 'sole basis of the revelation of the Messiah in the New Testament is the Old Testament.' Thus the details of the birth narratives, the identifications between John the Baptist and Elijah, between Joshua and Jesus, Miriam and Mary, indicate that for every type there is an antitype. Correspondences abound: Hannah's song and that glorious communist manifesto we call the Magnificat together form an obvious example of such typology. There are 'great difficulties here for the single vision: none whatsoever for a metaphorical language in which the paradox of "is and is not" is functional.' Once we get clear of the bind of 'either-or' and enter into the possibilities of 'both-and,' biblical typology makes considerably more sense.

Northrop Frye was a dedicated teacher. He chose to remain throughout his career in the department of English at Victoria University, a church-related institution within the University of Toronto. His generosity to undergraduates was a source of wonder; no question, however naïve, went without respectful response, often with surprises of disclosure. With similar commitment, he accepted invitations from people in other fields. One of his last public lectures was to the medical staff of Toronto's Mount Sinai Hospital. Frye found his white-coated listeners less jaded and inhibited than many he had encountered in academe, and even he was startled by the spontaneity and enthusiasm around him. During an explication of the myths of freedom and concern, a young medical student could no longer contain himself; he leapt to his feet and shouted 'Right on!' This large audience – from junior to most senior staff – was hungry for Frye's ideas and he, in turn, was rejuvenated by their exuberance. I was present with others of Frye's colleagues, watching our professor delight once again in educating the imagination. Since he consistently attributed his writing to questions asked by undergraduates, it may well be that some of the issues from that day are addressed in this book, which he was preparing at that very time. Frye rarely seemed happier than when he was going about his proper business of demystifying and democratizing knowledge among eager students.

Throughout his work, Frye used the term *spiritual* with amazing confidence as well as grace. This was certainly so for the colleagues to whom these three lectures were first addressed and for whom the final chapter was written, the alumni-ae of Emmanuel College, the theological faculty of Victoria University. Northrop Frye himself was a graduate of this institution, and like most of these women and men was an ordained minister of The United Church of Canada. Frye never obscured this connection and even enjoyed the jibe about working as its undercover agent. Increasingly, a number of critics, unable to reconcile the many facets of Frye, and impatient with the tradition that he enhanced and carried forward, attempted to undermine his system and its far-flung social impact. It became fashionable to refer to Frye as a *clergyman*, thereby attempting to undermine his credibility as a literary theorist. One critic, for example, managed to turn *parentheses* around 'Frye is a clergyman' into *emphases* to explain away summarily any value that his literary theories might otherwise possess: 'Frye offers literature as a displaced version of religion.' Other detractors derided what they called Frye's 'middle-class liberal values.' All this came as no surprise to Frye, who knew full well that Good Friday follows Palm Sunday. He had a well-tempered response to those who attacked his system. As he explained in a keynote address at a conference on computers, he refused to see literary theories as competing theories but viewed them simply as 'different programs' for looking at the same reality. One of the most satisfying aspects of *The Double Vision* is that Frye deals very well with the trivialization and reduction of his thought, and we can rejoice that these lectures have given him the opportunity to have the last word on his subject.

With malice toward none, Frye defends his church against those who demand absolute certainties, replying simply that we do not pretend to know what nobody actually *knows* anyway. The sham and pretence of much that passes for religion is thus neatly exposed. Frye has often remarked that when one person says to another, 'You must believe in God,' what is really meant is 'You must believe in what I mean by God.' As Frye sees it, the trickster-god who makes deals and delights in bears-eating-children is a product of the demonic side of human invention; the God of love who can redeem time and our puny preoccupations is the God of the human imagination reaching as far as it can go. Frye does not hide from himself or his church the horrors of its history – of terror, intolerance, and hatred – a history we must outgrow. 'The real reformation toward a more mature society of individualized Christians was betrayed by Protestants as well as opposed by Catholics.' He cherished Auden's words, 'We must love one another or die.' Frye thinks that 'immense changes could be brought about by a Christianity that was no longer a ghost with the chains of a foul historical record of cruelty clanking behind it, that was no longer crippled by notions of heresy, infallibility, or exclusiveness of a kind that should be totally renounced and not rationalized to the slightest degree.' Frye, speaking as a Christian, says, 'When we encounter a vision quite different "from our own" in, say, a Buddhist, a Jew, a Confucian, an atheist or whatever, there can still be what is called dialogue, and mutual understanding, based on a sense that there is plenty of room in the mind of God for us both. All faith is founded on good faith. And where there is good faith on both sides there is also the presence of God.'

One of the declared purposes of *The Double Vision* is 'to clean up the human picture of God.' The author of our being becomes our only possible role model – 'one who comes eating and drinking,' who valuing his own privacy is yet a suffering servant totally concerned with the world without desiring any power in it except over his own person. Using our narrative scriptures of metaphors and myths to live by, Frye seems to be suggesting that the church in which he was an ordained minister not only stands *for* something but has in it the imagination to stand *by* anyone of any persuasion through the medium of good faith.

In his preface to this book, Frye refers to its contents as one believer at a 'rest stop' in his pilgrimage, 'however near that pilgrimage may now be to its close.' Between the writing of *The Double Vision* and its publication fell the shadow, and so this book takes on a new poignancy and intensity. The confluence of the death of the author with the birth of his last creation points us to that aspect of the imagination that can lift us clear of time, which Frye has described as the enemy of all living things, into an eternal present. Frye recognized our need for improved binoculars, that within each of us there are at least two readers. The single vision (of language, nature, history, and God) is an impoverished one leading to the destruction of everything that makes human or divine sense. The double vision, however, releases our imaginative and creative energy to see through our own minds and hearts that all things, through love, are possible.

Frye has called simile and metaphor not the ornaments of language but its elements. His own similes come often from music, and his metaphors dependably come from poetry. There may be a 'sudden rightness' then in placing the last four lectures of Northrop Frye beside the *Last Songs* of composer Richard Strauss and the *Four Quartets* of poet T.S. Eliot. The golden longing for peace is present in them all. 'Little Gidding' for Eliot, like the final song for Strauss, and 'The Double Vision of God,' Frye's final chapter, shapes and makes more complete sense of the first three compositions:

> We shall not cease from exploration
> And the end of all our exploring
> Will be to arrive where we started
> And know the place for the first time
>
> Quick now, here, now, always –
> A condition of complete simplicity
> (Costing not less than everything)
> And all shall be well
> And all manner of things shall be well
> When the tongues of flame are in-folded
> Into the crowned knot of fire
> And the fire and the rose are one.

In Eliot's affirmation of the death that makes sense of life, the disparate elements of the twilight zone of existence are seen at last in their true forms in the double vision of fire and rose. At the conclusion of his final essay in this book, Frye assures us that 'in the double vision of a spiritual and physical world simultaneously present, every moment we have lived through we have also died out of into another order. Our life in the resurrection, then, is already here, and waiting to be recognized.'

The Double Vision is rooted within the inclusive traditions of a Canadian reformation church as well as in the thought of one of its finest minds. It frees us to glimpse the double visions of language, nature, history, and even God – accepting that 'the mystery behind knowledge is not darkness but shadow.'

Johan L. Aitken
University of Toronto
February 1991

Preface

The first three chapters of this book were delivered as lectures at the Emmanuel College alumni reunion on 14, 15, and 16 May 1990 at Emmanuel College. Although various lectures of mine that were addressed specifically to Victoria College are in print (e.g., *No Uncertain Sounds* 1988), this is my first publication devoted specifically to Emmanuel College. I was very pleased that the lectures coincided with Douglas Jay's final year as principal, and consequently can be regarded as in part a tribute to him.

I say in part, because I had also hoped to make this small book something of a shorter and more accessible version of the longer books, *The Great Code* and *Words with Power*, that I have written on the relations of the Bible to secular culture. Many passages from the longer books are echoed here, in what I hope is a somewhat simpler context. After writing the lectures out in their final form, however, it seemed to me that the total argument implied by them was still incomplete, and I have therefore, after considerable hesitation, added a fourth chapter.

The fact that these lectures were addressed by a member of The United Church of Canada to a largely United Church audience accounts for many of the allusions, for some of the directions in the argument, and for much of the tone. As is utterly obvious, they represent the opinions of one member of that church only. And even those opinions should not be read as proceeding from a judgment seat of final conviction, but from a rest stop on a pilgrimage, however near the pilgrimage may now be to its close.

N.F.
Victoria University
University of Toronto
July 1990

The Double Vision

Chapter One

The Double Vision
of Language

The Whirligig of Time, 1925–90

I begin with a date. In 1990 The United Church of Canada, founded in 1925, reached an age often associated with superannuation. Only a minority of its members now recall church union, and there are still fewer who acquired, as I did, their elementary religious training within the pre-union Methodist church. In Methodism, even of the episcopal variety to which my family belonged, there was an emphasis on religious experience as distinct from doctrine and on very early exposure to the story element in the Bible. Such a conditioning may have helped to propel me in the direction of a literary criticism that has kept revolving around the Bible, not as a source of doctrine but as a source of story and vision. It may be of interest to explain what effect I think this has had on my general point of view on the world today, apart from the peculiar features of what I have written.

History moves in a cyclical rhythm which never forms a complete or closed cycle. A new movement begins, works itself out to exhaustion, and something of the original state then reappears, though in a quite new context presenting new conditions. I have lived through at least one major historical cycle of this kind: its main outlines are familiar to you, but the inferences I have drawn from it may be less so. When I arrived at Victoria College as a freshman in September 1929, North

America was not only prosperous but in a nearly hysterical state of self-congratulation. It was widely predicted that the end of poverty and the levelling out of social inequalities were practically within reach. In the Soviet Union, on the other hand, the reports were mainly of misery and despair. The inference for general public opinion on this side of the Atlantic was clear: capitalism worked and Marxism didn't.

Next month came the stock market crash, and there was no more talk of a capitalist Utopia. By the mid-thirties the climate of opinion had totally reversed, at least in the student circles I was attached to. Then it was a generally accepted dogma that capitalism had had its day and was certain to evolve very soon, with or without a revolution, into socialism, socialism being assumed to be both a more efficient and a morally superior system. The persistence of this view helped to consolidate my own growing feeling that myths are the functional units of human society, even when they are absurd myths. The myth in this case was the ancient George and dragon one: fascism was the dragon, democracy the maiden to be rescued, and despite the massacres, the deliberately organized famines, the mass uprooting of peoples, the grabbing of neighbouring territories, and the concentration camps, Stalin simply had to fit into the role of the rescuing knight. This was by no means a unanimous feeling – among Communists themselves there was a bitterly anti-Stalin Trotskyite group – but it extended over a good part of the left of centre.

That cycle has completed itself, and once again people in the West are saying, as they said sixty years ago, that it has been proved that capitalism works and that Marxism does not. With the decline of belief in Marxism, apart from an intellectual minority in the West that doesn't have to live with it, the original Marxist vision is often annexed by the opposite camp. Going back to the competitive economy that Marx denounced, we are often told, will mean a new life for the human race, perhaps even the ultimate goal that Marx himself promised: an end to exploitation and class struggle. Hope springs eternal: unfortunately it usually springs prematurely.

The failure of communism, or what has been assumed to be

communism – it was more accurately a form of state capitalism – is apparently a genuine failure, but it would be silly to return to the 1929 naïveté. Marxist economies may be trying to survive by making extensive reforms in an open-market direction, but capitalism only survived the last half-century by abandoning the more nihilistic aspects of laissez-faire and making equally extensive reforms in a socialist and welfare-state direction. For all the see-sawing between nationalizing and privatizing, the permanent effects of the Roosevelt revolution in the United States, and parallel revolutions in Western Europe, make it impossible to put any confidence in back-to-square-one clichés.

In capitalism there is both a democratic and an oligarchic tendency, and the moral superiority of capitalism over communism depends entirely on the ascendancy of the democratic element. Most citizens in North America, at least from about 1945 on, were only subliminally aware of living under a capitalist system: what mattered to them was political democracy, not the economic structure. Similarly, news analysts today put their main emphasis on the growing disillusionment with all forms of ideology in Eastern Europe, and the emerging feeling that systems do not matter: it is only freedom and dignity and the elementary amenities of civilization that matter. The view of Hegel that history was progressing through conflicts of ideas toward an ultimate goal of freedom was reversed by Marx into a view of history that identified the conflicting elements with materialistic forces, especially instruments of production and the class struggle over their ownership. Through a good deal of the twentieth century, it was generally assumed, even in the non-Marxist world, that Hegel's main contribution to philosophy was in getting his construct stood on its head by Marx. But now the original Hegelian conception is being revived, and the revolutions of our day are sometimes seen as manifestations of an impulse to freedom that may put an end to history as we have known it.

Freedom alone, however, is far too abstract a goal. As Heine said, freedom is a prison song: those who care about it are those who have been deprived of it. History tells us that, ever since

Adam's six hours in paradise, man has never known what to do with freedom except throw it away. Involved in the Christian conception of original sin is the perception that no human society is likely to do anything sensible for longer than the time that it takes to break a New Year's resolution. Despite this, I think there is a real truth in the notion of an impulse to freedom, but it needs to be placed in a broader and more practical context.

Human beings are concerned beings, and it seems to me that there are two kinds of concern: primary and secondary. Primary concerns are such things as food, sex, property, and freedom of movement: concerns that we share with animals on a physical level. Secondary concerns include our political, religious, and other ideological loyalties. All through history ideological concerns have taken precedence over primary ones. We want to live and love, but we go to war; we want freedom, but depend on the exploiting of other peoples, of the natural environment, even of ourselves. In the twentieth century, with a pollution that threatens the supply of air to breathe and water to drink, it is obvious that we cannot afford the supremacy of ideological concerns any more. The need to eat, love, own property, and move about freely must come first, and such needs require peace, good will, and a caring and responsible attitude to nature. A continuing of ideological conflict, a reckless exploiting of the environment, a persistence in believing, with Mao Tse-Tung, that power comes out of the barrel of a gun, would mean, quite simply, that the human race cannot be long for this world.

The Cold War gave us a Soviet Union upholding an allegedly materialistic ideology, at the price of chronic food shortages, sexual prudery, abolition of all property except the barest essentials of clothing and shelter, and a rigidly repressed freedom of movement. The United States offered vast quantities of food and drink, indiscriminate sexual activity, piling up of excessive wealth and privilege, and a restless nomadism – in other words, full satisfaction of primary concerns on a purely physical level. An evolution toward freedom, however, is conceivable if freedom is a primary concern, if it belongs in the context of enough to eat and drink, of normal sexual satisfaction, of enough clothing, shelter, and property.

The immediate concern of freedom is still a physical one: it is a matter of being able to move about without being challenged by policemen demanding passports and permits and identity cards, and of not being excluded from occupations and public places on the ground of sex or skin colour. I should explain also that when I speak of property I mean the external forms of what is 'proper' to one's life as an individual, starting with clothing and shelter. These also include what may be called territorial space. A Hindu hermit meditating in a forest may need next to nothing of clothing and shelter, and no possessions at all, but he still needs space around him.

The United States, Japan, and Western Europe have been much more successful in achieving stage one of primary concern: as compared with the formerly Marxist countries, they are more attractive and more comfortable to live in. But the legacy of the Cold War is still with us, and not only does an adversarial situation impoverish both sides, but both sides catch the worst features of their opponents. We have seen this in the McCarthyism that imitated the Stalinist show trials, the McCarran act that imitated Soviet exclusion policies, and the interventions in Latin America that imitate the Stalinist attitude to the Warsaw Pact countries. Something, at the very least, is still missing.

Primitive and Mature Societies

When Jesus was tempted by the devil to improve the desert economy by turning stones into bread, he answered, quoting Deuteronomy, that man shall not live by bread alone, but by prophecies as well. That is, primary concerns, for conscious human beings, must have a spiritual as well as a physical dimension. Freedom of movement is not simply the freedom to take a plane to Vancouver; it must include freedom of thought and criticism. Similarly, property should extend to scientific discovery and the production of poetry and music; sex should be a matter of love and companionship and not a frenetic rutting in rubber; food and drink should become a focus of the sharing of goods within a community. I pass over the violence, the drug addiction, and the general collapse of moral standards that accompany overemphasis on the satisfying of physical wants, because one hardly needs to be told that they are the result of a lack of spiritual vision. The obvious question to raise next is, What is the difference between the spiritual aspect of primary concerns and the secondary or ideological concerns just mentioned?

I think the difference is expressed in two types of society, one primitive and the other mature. A primitive or embryonic society is one in which the individual is thought of as primarily a function of the social group. In all such societies a hierarchical structure of authority has to be set up to ensure that the individual does not get too far out of line. A mature society, in contrast, understands that its primary aim is to develop a genuine individuality in its members. In a fully mature society the structure of authority becomes a function of the individuals within it, all of them, without distinctions of sex, class, or race, living, loving, thinking, and producing with a sense of space around them. Throughout history practically all societies have been primitive ones in our present sense: a greater maturity and a genuine concern for the individual peeps out occasionally, but is normally smothered as society collapses back again into its primitive form.

The reason for this is that we all belong to something before we are anything, and the primitive structure has all the vast power of human inertia and passive social conditioning on its side. Fifty years ago, the great appeal of Marxism to intellectuals in the West was that it renewed the emphasis on primitive social values, providing a social gospel with the right answers in what purported to be not only a rational but a scientific system. Many conservatives of that time preferred a similar structure that some Roman Catholic intellectuals believed they had discovered in Thomist realism; people who simply hated human intelligence turned fascist. In the United States only a minority wanted to buy any of these nostrums, but the Americans had their own primitive mattress to sleep on, the American way of life, with all its anti-intellectual cosiness.

What I am expounding may be called a bourgeois liberal view, which throughout my lifetime has never been regarded as an 'advanced' view. But it may begin to look more central with the repudiation of Marxism in Marxist countries, the growing uneasiness with the anti-intellectualism in American life, and the steadily decreasing dividends of terrorism in Third World countries. The ascendant feeling in Eastern Europe now is that a collective ideology is no longer good enough for human dignity. What triggered the feeling, we said, was the failure of communism to provide the physical basis of primary concern: food, possessions, and free movement. Even on the physical level, primary concerns are still individual: famine is a social problem, but it is the individual who eats or starves. But the spiritual form of these concerns is the sign of the real failure.

The spiritual form of primary concern, then, fulfils the physical need but incorporates it into the context of an individualized society. The ideological or secondary concern may be the same in theory, but its subordination of individual to social needs constantly frustrates, postpones, or circumvents the fulfilment of the primary ones. Where there is no awareness of such a distinction there are often arguments, in cultural circles particularly, contrasting socially engaged and activist art, where every book or film or picture is or should be a political statement, with introverted or ingrown creativity that concentrates on subjective feelings. The antithesis is false because it is an antithesis: in a mature culture it would disappear.

I said that an adversarial situation like that of the Cold War impoverishes both sides. The one adversarial situation that does not do so is the conflict between the demands of primary human welfare on the one hand, and a paranoid clinging to arbitrary power on the other. Naturally this black-and-white situation is often very hard to find in the complexities of revolutions and power struggles, but it is there, and nothing in any revolutionary situation is of any importance except preserving it. When we see it, we can realize that the difference between ideological and spiritual concern is, among other things, a difference in language. Before I can clarify this point I must turn to the confrontation of primitive and mature social impulses in the history of religion.

Religious organizations are much more bound than the better secular ones to what I have called the primitive form of society, the supremacy of social authority over the individual. It frequently appears to be practically an element of faith that the interests and reputation of the church as a social unit must take precedence over the welfare of the individuals within it, a faith rationalized by the claim that the two things are always identical. Church authorities appeal to a revelation from God, or a corresponding spiritual power beyond the reach of revolutionary uprisings, of which they are the custodians and definitive interpreters. In many respects the twentieth-century Cold War repeated the later stages of the situation that arose with the Reformation in the sixteenth century. Then, a revolutionary movement, at first directed mainly toward a reform of abuses in the church, showed signs of expanding and breaking open a tightly closed structure of authority that claimed exclusive and infallible powers in both spiritual and temporal orders. What was centrally at issue was reformation itself, the conception of a church that could be reformed in principle and not merely through modifying the corruptions that had grown up within it. The Reformers thought of the church as subject to a higher criterion, namely the Word of God, and as obligated to carry on a continuous dialogue with the Word while in a subordinate position to it.

Established authority reacted to this movement as established authority invariably does. The Council of Trent gives an impression of passing one reactionary resolution after another in a spirit of the blindest panic. Yet the Council of Trent succeeded in its main objective, which was to persuade Catholics that post-Tridentine Catholicism was not only the legitimate descendant of the pre-Reformation church, but was in fact identical with it. The logical inference was the claim of a power of veto over the

Bible, a position set out in Newman's *Essay on the Development of Christian Doctrine*, where a historical dialectic takes supreme command in a way closely parallel to the constructs of Hegel and Marx.

There was also, of course, the argument that basing the church on justification by faith alone would lead to the chaos of private judgment and subjective relativism. What is important here is not the validity of such an argument but the fact that the main Reformed bodies tended to adopt it. When it came to establishing the Word of God as an authority, the Reformers themselves could only become the accredited spokesmen of that authority. And so the real reformation towards a more mature society of individualized Christians was betrayed by Protestants as well as opposed by Catholics. A historian might see the Lutheran and Anabaptist movements as primarily emphasizing different aspects of reformation, but Luther himself showed the same enthusiasm for killing off Anabaptists that, in the twentieth century, Communists showed for killing off Anarchists.

Many of the greatest spirits of Luther's time, such as Erasmus, looked for a movement toward a far greater spiritual maturity than either Reformation or Counter-Reformation achieved, and tried to hold to the standards of a liberalism that would transcend both the Roman Catholic status quo and its Lutheran and Calvinist antitheses. But for Erasmus, or for Rabelais, there was no attraction in a more hardened and sectarian version of what was already there.

So both sides took the broad way to destruction, with the bloody conflicts of civil wars in France and Germany, along with a war of Protestants fighting each other in Britain. In the course of centuries the adversarial situation gradually subsided into a cold war instead of actual war, which, however, did not eliminate, any more than its counterparts have eliminated in our day, endless persecution within individual nations. This cold war situation lasted roughly until our own time, when Vatican Two and ecumenical movements in Protestantism have begun to show how out of touch such antagonisms are with both the conditions of contemporary life and the spirit of Christianity. Religious parallels to the current political demands for greater individual autonomy sprang up in the more liberal Protestant circles in the nineteenth century and are now breaking into Catholicism on all sides, though still officially inadmissible to the upper hierarchy.

In the course of time the movement begun by the Reformation did achieve one major victory: the gradual spread throughout the Western world of the principle of separation of church and state. Something of the genuine secular benefits of democracy have rubbed off on the religious groups, to the immense benefit of humanity, and depriving religion of all secular or temporal power is one of the most genuinely emancipating movements of our time. It seems to be a general rule that the more 'orthodox' or 'fundamentalist' a religious attitude is, the more strongly it resents this separation and the more consistently it lobbies for legislation giving its formulas secular authority. Today, in Israel and in much of the Moslem and Hindu world, as well as in Northern Ireland and South Africa, we can clearly see that these religious attitudes are the worst possible basis for a secular society.

This principle applies equally to the dogmatic atheism and the anti-religious campaigns that Lenin assumed to be essential to the Marxist revolution. I was in Kiev during the celebration of the thousandth anniversary of the introduction of Christianity to Ukraine, and it was clear that seventy years of anti-religious propaganda had been as total and ignominious a failure there as anything in the economic or political sphere. In short, any religion, including atheism, which remains on the socially and psychologically primitive level, in the sense I have given to the word primitive, can do little more than illustrate Swift's gloomy axiom that men have only enough religion to hate each other but not enough for even a modicum of tolerance, let alone anything resembling charity.

Michael explains to Adam, in the last book of Milton's *Paradise Lost*, that tyranny exists in human society because every individual in such a society is a tyrant within himself, or at least is if he conforms acceptably to his social surroundings. The well-adjusted individual in a primitive society is composed of what

Paul calls the *soma psychikon*, or what the King James Bible translates as the 'natural man' (I Corinthians 2:14). He has, or thinks he has, a soul, or mind, or consciousness, sitting on top of certain impulses and desires that are traditionally called 'bodily.' 'Body' is a very muddled metaphor in this context: we should be more inclined today to speak of repressed elements in the psyche. In any case the natural man sets up a hierarchy within himself and uses his waking consciousness to direct and control his operations. We call him the natural man partly because he is, first, a product of nature, and inherits along with his genetic code the total devotion to his own interests that one writer has called 'the selfish gene.'

Second, he is a product of his social and ideological conditioning. He cannot distinguish what he believes from what he believes he believes, because his faith is simply an adherence to the statements of belief provided for him by social authority, whether spiritual or temporal. As with all hierarchies, the lower parts are less well adjusted than the upper ones, and 'underneath' in the restless and squirming body, or whatever else we call it, is a rabble of doubts telling him that his intellectual set-up is largely fraudulent. He may shout down his doubts and trample them underfoot as temptations coming from a lower world, but he is still what Hegel calls an unhappy consciousness.

For reassurance, he looks around him at the society which reflects his hierarchy in a larger order. A society composed of natural men is also a hierarchy in which there are superiors and inferiors, and if such a society has any stability, one draws a sense of security from one's social position, even if it is 'inferior.' Discontented inferiors, of course, are the social counterpart of doubts, and also have to be trampled underfoot. It is easy to see why the two most influential thinkers of the twentieth century are Marx and Freud: they were those who called attention, in the social and the individual spheres respectively, to the exploitation in society, to the latent hysteria in the individual, and to the alienation produced by both.

Inside one's natural and social origin, however, is the embryo of a genuine individual struggling to be born. But this unborn individual is so different from the natural man that Paul has to call it by a different name. The New Testament sees the genuine human being as emerging from an embryonic state within nature and society into the fully human world of the individual, which is symbolized as a rebirth or second birth, in the phrase that Jesus used to Nicodemus. Naturally this rebirth cannot mean any separation from one's natural and social context, except insofar as a greater maturity includes some knowledge of the conditioning that was formerly accepted uncritically. The genuine human being thus born is the *soma pneumatikon*, the spiritual body (I Corinthians 15:44). This phrase means that spiritual man is a body: the natural man or *soma psychikon* merely has one. The resurrection of the spiritual body is the completion of the kind of life the New Testament is talking about, and to the extent that any society contains spiritual people, to that extent it is a mature rather than a primitive society.

The Crisis in Language

What concerns me in this situation is a linguistic fallacy, the fallacy that relates to the phrase 'literally true.' Ordinarily, we mean by 'literally true' what is descriptively accurate. We read many books for the purpose of acquiring information about the world outside the books we are reading, and we call what we read 'true' if it seems to be a satisfactory verbal replica of the information we seek. This conception of literal meaning as descriptive works only on the basis of sense experience and the logic that connects its data. That is, it works in scientific and historical writing. But it took a long time before such descriptive meaning could be fully mature and developed, because it depends on technological aids. We cannot describe phenomena accurately in science before we have the apparatus to do so; there cannot be a progressive historical knowledge until we have a genuine historiography, with access to documents and, for the earlier periods at least, some help from archaeology. Literalism of this kind in the area of the spiritual instantly becomes what Paul calls the letter that kills. It sets up an imitation of descriptive language, a pseudo-objectivity related to something that isn't there.

In the early Christian centuries it was widely assumed that the basis of Christian faith was the descriptive accuracy of the historical events recorded in the New Testament and the infallibility of the logical arguments that interconnected them. This pseudo-literalism was presented as assertion without the evidence of sense experience, and belief became a self-hypnotizing process designed to eke out the insufficiency of evidence. The rational arguments used were assumed to have a compulsive power: if we accept this, then that must follow, and so on. A compelling dialectic based on the excluding of opposites is a militant use of words; but where there is no genuine basis in sense experience, it is only verbally rational: it is really rhetoric, seeking not proof but conviction and conversion. It is seldom, however, that anyone is convinced by an argument unless there are psychological sympathies within that open the gates to it. So when words failed, as they usually did, recourse was had to anathematizing those who held divergent views, and from there it was an easy step to the psychosis of heresy-hunting, of regarding all deviation from approved doctrine as a malignant disease that had to be ruthlessly stamped out.

I am, of course, isolating only one element in Christianity, but cruelty, terror, intolerance, and hatred within any religion always mean that God has been replaced by the devil, and such things are always accompanied by a false kind of literalism. At present some other religions, notably Islam, are even less reassuring than our own. As Marxist and American imperialisms decline, the Moslem world is emerging as the chief threat to world peace, and the spark-plug of its intransigence, so to speak, is its fundamentalism or false literalism of belief. The same principle of demonic perversion applies here: when Khomeini gave the order to have Salman Rushdie murdered, he was turning the whole of the Koran into Satanic verses. In our own culture, Margaret Atwood's *The Handmaid's Tale* depicts a future New England in which a reactionary religious movement has brought back the hysteria, bigotry, and sexual sadism of seventeenth-century Puritanism. Such a development may seem unlikely just now, but the potential is all there.

For the last fifty years I have been studying literature, where the organizing principles are myth, that is, story or narrative, and metaphor, that is, figured language. Here we are in a completely liberal world, the world of the free movement of the spirit. If we read a story there is no pressure to believe in it or act upon it; if we encounter metaphors in poetry, we need not worry about their factual absurdity. Literature incorporates our ideological concerns, but it devotes itself mainly to the primary ones, in both physical and spiritual forms: its fictions show human beings in the primary throes of surviving, loving, prospering, and fighting with the frustrations that block these things. It is at once a world of relaxation, where even the most terrible tragedies are still called plays, and a world of far greater intensity than ordinary life affords. In short it does everything that can be done for people except transform them. It creates a world that the spirit can live in, but it does not make us spiritual beings.

It would be absurd to see the New Testament as only a work of literature: it is all the more important, therefore, to realize that it is written in the language of literature, the language of myth and metaphor. The Gospels give us the life of Jesus in the form of myth: what they say is, 'This is what happens when the Messiah comes to the world.' One thing that happens when the Messiah comes to the world is that he is despised and rejected, and searching in the nooks and crannies of the gospel text for a credibly historical Jesus is merely one more excuse for despising and rejecting him. Myth is neither historical nor anti-historical: it is counter-historical. Jesus is not presented as a historical figure, but as a figure who drops into history from another dimension of reality, and thereby shows what the limitations of the historical perspective are.

The gospel confronts us with all kinds of marvels and mysteries, so that one's initial reaction may very well be that what we are reading is fantastic and incredible. Biblical scholars have a distinction here ready to hand, the distinction between world history and sacred history, *Weltgeschichte* and *Heilsgeschichte*. Unfortunately, there is as yet almost no understanding of what sacred history is, so the usual procedure is to try to squeeze everything possible into ordinary history, with the bulges of the incredible that still stick out being smoothed away by a process called demythologizing. However, the Gospels are all myth and all bulge, and the operation does not work.

As the New Testament begins with the myth of the Messiah, so it ends, in the Book of Revelation, with the metaphor of the Messiah, the vision of all things in their infinite variety united in the body of Christ. And just as myth is not anti-historical but counter-historical, so the metaphor, the statement or implication that two things are identical though different, is neither logical nor illogical, but counter-logical. It presents the continuous paradox of experience, in which whatever one meets both is and is not oneself. 'I am a part of all that I have met,' says Tennyson's Ulysses; 'I am what is around me,' says Wallace Stevens. Metaphors are paradoxical, and again we suspect that perhaps only in paradox are words doing the best they can for us. The genuine Christianity that has survived its appalling historical record was founded on charity, and charity is invariably linked to an imaginative conception of language, whether consciously or unconsciously. Paul makes it clear that the language of charity is spiritual language, and that spiritual language is metaphorical, founded on the metaphorical paradox that we live in Christ and that Christ lives in us.

I am not trying to deny or belittle the validity of a credal, even a dogmatic, approach to Christianity: I am saying that the literal basis of faith in Christianity is a mythical and metaphorical basis, not one founded on historical facts or logical propositions. Once we accept an imaginative literalism, everything else falls into place: without that, creeds and dogmas quickly turn malignant. The literary language of the New Testament is not intended, like literature itself, simply to suspend judgment, but to convey a vision of spiritual life that continues to transform and expand our own. That is, its myths become, as purely literary myths cannot, myths to live by; its metaphors become, as purely literary metaphors cannot, metaphors to live in. This transforming power is sometimes called kerygma or proclamation. Kerygma in this sense is again a rhetoric, but a rhetoric coming the other way and coming from the other side of mythical and metaphorical language.

In the Book of Job we have the rhetorical speech of Elihu, defending and justifying the ways of God; then we have the proclamation of God himself, couched in very similar language, but reversed in direction. The proclamation of the gospel is closely associated with the myths that we call parables, because teaching by myth and metaphor is the only way of educating a free person in spiritual concerns. If we try to eliminate the literal basis of kerygma in myth and metaphor, everything goes wrong again, and we are back where we started, in the rhetoric of an all-too-human effort to demonstrate the essence of revelation. The reason for basing kerygma on mythical and metaphorical language is that such a language is the only one with the power to detach us from the world of facts and demonstrations and reasonings, which are excellent things as tools, but are merely idols as objects of trust and reverence.

Demonic literalism seeks conquest by paralyzing argument; imaginative literalism seeks what might be called interpenetration, the free flowing of spiritual life into and out of one another that communicates but never violates. As Coleridge said (unless Schelling said it first), 'The medium by which spirits understand each other is not the surrounding air, but the *freedom* which they possess in common.' As the myths and metaphors of Scripture gradually become, for us, myths and metaphors that we can live by and in, that not only work for us but constantly expand our horizons, we may enter the world of proclamation and pass on to others what we have found to be true for ourselves. When we encounter a quite different vision in, say, a Buddhist, a Jew, a Confucian, an atheist, or whatever, there can still be what is called dialogue, and mutual understanding, based on a sense that there is plenty of room in the mind of God for us both. All faith is founded on good faith, and where there is good faith on both sides there is also the presence of God.

The same thing is true of variations of belief among Christians. Some prominent cleric may announce, after much heart-searching and self-harrowing, that he can no longer 'believe in' the Virgin Birth. What he thinks he is saying is that he can no longer honestly accept the historicity of the nativity stories in Matthew and Luke. But those stories do not belong to ordinary history at all: they form part of *Heilsgeschichte*, a mythical narrative containing many features that cannot be assimilated to the historian's history. What he is really saying is that some elements in the gospel myth have less transforming power for him than others. His version of Christianity could never have built a cathedral to Notre Dame de Chartres or written the hymn to the Virgin at the end of Dante's *Paradiso*, but his version is his, and that is his business only. However, if he had been a better educated cleric he would not have raised the point in the wrong context and created false issues.

The Epistle to the Hebrews says that faith is the *hypostasis* of the hoped-for and the *elenchos* or proof of the unseen. That is, faith is the reality of hope and of illusion. In this sense faith starts with a vision of reality that is something other than history or logic, which accepts the world as it is, and on the basis of that vision it can begin to remake the world. A nineteenth-century disciple of Kant, Hans Vaihinger, founded a philosophy on the phrase 'as if,' and the literal basis of faith from which we should start, the imaginative and poetic basis, is a fiction we enter into 'as if' it were true. There is no certainty in faith to begin with: we are free to deny the reality of the spiritual challenge of the New Testament, and if we accept it we accept it tentatively, taking a risk. The certainty comes later, and very gradually, with the growing sense in our own experience that the vision really does have the power that it claims to have.

I use the word 'risk' advisedly: I am not minimizing the difficulties and dangers of an imaginative literalism. All through history there has run a distrust and contempt for imaginative language, and the words for story or literary narrative – myth, fable, and fiction – have all acquired a secondary sense of falsehood or something made up out of nothing. Overcoming this perversion of language takes time and thought, and besides, there are as many evil myths and vicious metaphors as there are evil doctrines and vicious arguments. But the author of Hebrews goes on to talk, in the examples he gives after his definition of faith, about the risks taken by vision, and he suggests that such risks are guided by more effective powers than merely subjective ones. Besides, we are not alone: we live not only in God's world but in a community with a tradition behind it. Preserving the inner vitality of that community and that tradition is what the churches are for.

I have been trying to suggest a basis for the openness of belief that is characteristic of the United Church. Many of you will still recall an article in a Canadian journal that emphasized this openness, and drew the conclusion that the United Church was now an 'agnostic' church. I think the writer was trying to be fair-minded, but his conclusion was nonsense: the United Church is agnostic only in the sense that it does not pretend to know what nobody actually 'knows' anyway. The article quoted a church member as asking, If a passage in Scripture fails to transform me, is it still true? The question was a central one, but it reminded me of a story told me by a late colleague who many years ago was lecturing on Milton's view of the Trinity. He explained the difference between Athanasian and Arian positions, and how Milton, failing to find enough scriptural evidence for the Athanasian position, adopted a qualified or semi-Arian one. He was interrupted by a student who said impatiently, 'But I want to know the truth about the Trinity.' One may sympathize with the student, but trying to satisfy him is futile. What 'the' truth is, is not available to human beings in spiritual matters: the goal of our spiritual life is God, who is a spiritual Other, not a spiritual object, much less a conceptual object. That is why the Gospels keep reminding us how many listen and how few hear: truths of the gospel kind cannot be demonstrated except through personal example. As the seventeenth-century Quaker Isaac Penington said, every truth is substantial in its own place, but all truths are shadows except the last. The language that lifts us clear of the merely plausible and the merely credible is the language of the spirit; the language of the spirit is, Paul tells us, the language of love, and the language of love is the only language that we can be sure is spoken and understood by God.

Chapter Two

The Double Vision
of Nature

Natural and Human Societies

I have taken my title 'The Double Vision' from a phrase in a poem of Blake incorporated in a letter to Thomas Butts (22 November 1802):

> For double the vision my eyes do see,
> And a double vision is always with me:
> With my inward eye 'tis an old man grey;
> With my outward a thistle across my way.

The surface meaning of this appears to be that Blake is adding a subjective hallucination to the sense perception of an object, and that adding this hallucination is what makes him the visionary poet and painter that he is. If this is what Blake is saying, he is talking nonsense, and Blake very seldom talks nonsense. The general idea, however, seems to be that simple sense perception is not enough. We may be reminded of a well-known bit of doggerel from Wordsworth:

> A primrose by a river's brim
> A yellow primrose was to him,
> And it was nothing more.

Well, what more should it be? If I were a primrose by a river's brim, I should feel insulted.

Clearly a good deal depends on what is meant by 'more.' If it means something in addition to the perception of the primrose, we seem to be headed for some kind of deliberate program of disorganizing sense experience of a type later proposed by Rimbaud, who said that the poet wishing to be a visionary must go through a long and systematic unsettling (*dérèglement*) of sense experience. But there seems to be something unreliable about this program, if it had anything to do with the fact that one of the greatest of French poets stopped writing when he was barely out of his teens. If, on the other hand, Wordsworth is simply speaking of seeing the primrose itself with a greater intensity, that may be part of a 'more' stable and continuous process.

We have to give the context of what Blake says at this point, as we shall be referring to it later. He has acquired, he tells us, a double-double or fourfold vision, although it is still essentially twofold, in contrast to what he prays to be delivered from:

> 'Tis fourfold in my supreme delight,
> And threefold in soft Beulah's night,
> And twofold always. May God us keep
> From single vision and Newton's sleep!

However paradoxical his language, Blake is not recommending that one should try to awaken from the sleep of single vision by seeing two objects instead of one, especially when one of the two is not there. I think he means rather that the conscious subject is not really perceiving until it recognizes itself as part of what it perceives. The whole world is humanized when such a perception takes place. There must be something human about the object, alien as it may at first seem, which the perceiver is relating to. The 'old man grey' is clearly an aspect of Blake himself, and stands for the fact that whatever we perceive is a part of us and forms an identity with us.

First, there is the world of the thistle, the world of nature presented directly to us. This is obviously the world within which our physical bodies have evolved, but from which consciousness feels oddly separated. Nature got along for untold ages without us: it could get along very well without us now and may again get along without us in the future. The systematic study of nature, which is the main business of science, reflects this sense of separation. It is impersonal, avoids value judgments and commitments to emotion or imagination, and confines itself to explanations that are largely in terms of mechanism. This is the view that Blake associates with the outlook of Isaac Newton, and although Newton was a religious man who saw many religious implications in his own science, there is a sense in which Blake was right. There is no God in the scientific vision as such: if we bring God into science, we turn him into a mechanical engineer, like the demiurge of Plato's *Timaeus* or the designing watch-maker God of the various Christian and deistic attempts at natural theology.

True, science has abandoned *narrowly* mechanistic explanations in one field after another since Blake spoke of Newton's sleep. It is sixty years since Sir James Jeans, in *The Mysterious Universe*, gave God a degree in mathematics rather than mechanical engineering, mathematics being a field that admits of paradox, even of irrationalities. It is an equally long time since Whitehead criticized the conception of 'simple location' that underlies Blake's polemic against single vision. But scientific explanations are still mainly non-teleological, confining themselves to the *how* of things, though there are signs that science may be coming to the end of this self-denying ordinance.

The first aspect of the double vision that we have to become aware of is the distinction between the natural and the human environment. There is the natural environment which is simply there, and is, in mythological language, our mother. And there is the human environment, the world we are trying to build out of the natural one. We think of the two worlds as equally real, though we spend practically our whole time in the human one. We wake up in the morning in our bedrooms, and feel that we have abolished an unreal world, the world of the dream, and are now in the world of waking reality. But everything surrounding us in that bedroom is a human artefact.

If science is more impersonal than literature or religion, that is the result of certain conventions imposed on science by its specific subject-matter. It studies the natural environment, but as part of the human constructed world. It discovers counterparts of the human sense of order and predictability in nature, and the scientist as human being would not differ psychologically from the artist in the way he approaches his work. The axiom of the eighteenth-century Italian philosopher Giambattista Vico was *verum factum*: we understand nothing except what we have made. Again, it is only the human environment that can be personal, and if God belongs in this distinction at all, he must, being a person, be sought for in the human world.

As the natural ancestry of human beings is not in dispute, it was inevitable that at some point the question should be raised of how far a 'natural society' is possible, and whether man could simply live in a state of harmony with nature, instead of withdrawing his consciousness from nature and devoting his energies to a separable order of existence. Such speculations arose mainly in the eighteenth century, in the age of Rousseau. They have not stood up very well to what anthropology has since gleaned from the study of primitive societies. There seems to be no human society that does not live within an envelope of law, ritual, custom, and myth that seals it off from nature, however closely its feeding and mating and hunting habits may approximate those of animals.

When our remote ancestors were tree opossums or whatever, avoiding the carnivorous dinosaurs, they were animals totally preoccupied, as other animals still are for the most part, with the primary concerns of food, sex, territory, and free movement on a purely physical level. With the dawn of consciousness humanity feels separated from nature and looks at it as something objective to itself. This is the starting point of Blake's single vision, where we no longer feel part of nature but are helplessly staring at it.

Thomas Pynchon's remarkable novel *Gravity's Rainbow* is a book that seems to me to have grasped a central principle of this situation. The human being, this novel tells us, is instinctively paranoid: We are first of all convinced that the world was expressly made for us and designed in detail for our benefit and appreciation. As soon as we are afflicted by doubts about this, we plunge into the other aspect of paranoia, feel that our environment is absurd and alienating, and that we are uniquely accursed in being aware, unlike any other organism in nature, of our own approaching mortality. Pynchon makes it clear that this paranoia can be and is transformed into creative energy and becomes the starting point of everything that humanity has done in the arts and sciences. But before it is thus transformed, it is the state that the Bible condemns as idolatry, in which we project numinous beings or forces into nature and scan nature anxiously for signs of its benevolence or wrath directed toward us.

The Bible is emphatic that nothing numinous exists in nature, that there may be devils there but no gods, and that nature is to be thought of as a fellow-creature of man. However, the paranoid attitude to nature that Pynchon describes survives in the manic-depressive psychosis of the twentieth century. In the manic phase, we are told that the age of Aquarius is coming, and that soon the world will be turned back to the state of innocence. In the depressive phase, news analysts explain that pollution has come to a point at which any sensible nature would simply wipe us out and start experimenting with a new species. In interviews I am almost invariably asked at some point whether I feel optimistic or pessimistic about some contemporary situation. The answer is that these imbecile words are euphemisms for manic-depressive highs and lows, and that anyone who struggles for sanity avoids both.

We do emerge, however, to some degree, from the illusions of staring at nature into building a human world of culture and civilization, and from that perspective we can see the natural environment as the 'material' world in the sense of providing the materials for our unique form of existence. Practically all of our made world represents a huge waste of effort: it includes the world of war, of cutthroat competition, of stagnating bureaucracies, of the lying and hypocrisy of what is called public relations. Above all, it has not achieved any genuine rapprochement with nature itself, but simply regards nature as an area of exploitation. Where God may belong in this duality we have yet to try to see, but as he is not hidden in nature, he can only be connected with that tiny percentage of human activity that has not been hopelessly botched.

The reason for this is that we have separated from nature but are still regarding it as a mirror of ourselves, from within the prison of Narcissus. In the state of nature there may well be a good deal of what the anarchist Kropotkin called, on the basis of the studies that he made of the subject, 'mutual aid.' But what are more obvious and picturesque in nature are the patterns of tyranny and anarchy that are constantly appealed to by rationalizers of bad social systems. The communities formed by animals are full of hierarchies and pecking orders, of females forcibly seized by stronger males, of fights over territorial disputes, and the like, even if they fall short of the total obliterating of the individual that we see in communities of social insects. There are patterns of laissez-faire anarchy, too, in the hunting of predators like the great jungle cats: calling the lion the 'king of beasts' helps to reassure us that a society in which the predators are the aristocracy is the right one for us as well.

But humanity's primary duty is not to be natural but to be human. The reason why idolatry is dangerous is that it suggests the attractiveness and the ease with which we may collapse into the preconscious state from which we have been trying to emerge. As long as idolatry persists, and humanity is seeing in nature a mirror of itself, it forms primitive societies (in the sense used earlier) as an imitation of nature. Nearly all human history shows one society after another sinking back into the order of nature as thus conceived, setting up regimes of tyranny and anarchy in which mere survival is all that is left of human life for the great majority. Human beings get along as best they can in such a world, but the human spirit knows that it is living in hell.

While humanity is continually sliding back into a state of nature to which it is totally unadapted, there is still a steady process of work that transforms the natural environment into a human one. In the Bible the images of this transformation, the flocks and herds of the animal world, the harvests and vintages, farms and gardens of the vegetable world, the buildings and highways made from the inorganic world, symbolize the fulfilling of what I call human primary concerns. This process is a social and communal enterprise, and if tyranny and exploitation are relaxed for a moment, the genuinely social virtues of cooperation and neighbourliness soon emerge. But the energy of social work, though certainly intelligent and conscious, tends also to be uncritical and instinctive.

Criticism and Civilization

In the nineteenth-century work that transformed Ontario from a forested environment into an agricultural one, there were many largely unexamined assumptions: the immense destruction of trees and slaughter of forest animals were necessary to 'clear' the land, and nothing else needed to be said about it. In the twentieth century a largely farming and small-town population was transformed into an urban one, a process again largely uncritical. But eventually certain crises, especially pollution and such questions as what to do with our garbage and sewage, force us into a criticism of what such work is doing. Here we have moved into a higher power of consciousness and a new dimension of concern.

In the construction of the human world we recognize two elements. One is the element of work, which is energy expended for a further end in view. The other is play, or energy expended for its own sake. In the animal world play seems to be important mainly to young animals, and to have the function there of a kind of rehearsal for more mature activities. In the human world play is more complex: it opens up a world of freedom and leisure out of which the typically human form of consciousness comes, and it produces the creative arts. In communities preoccupied with physical labour, the members of such communities are usually regarded as either manual workers or slackers, and the creative arts are often thought of as socially expendable, or even irresponsible. But just as the play of puppies indicates something of what they will be as grown dogs, so the creative arts set up models of what I have been calling primary concerns. Fiction and drama in literature, I have said, depict people making love, gaining property, wandering off on adventures, struggling to survive. Some aspects of literature, such as the comic and the romantic, lean in the direction of wish-fulfilment; the tragic and the ironic emphasize frustration and maladjustment. This latter especially means that in the verbal arts at least a creative and a critical element are inseparable. In fact Matthew Arnold even spoke of poetry as a criticism of life.

Every human society is mired in all the miseries of original sin, but we never fail to find something in its culture that is attractive, and not only attractive but communicable, speaking directly to us across the widest abysses of time or space or language. With simpler societies we find most of this sense of a kindred human spirit in what are called useful arts: pottery, textiles, basketwork and the like, which are preserved in museums for their potential cultural contact. It used to be that the fine arts were ranked above the useful arts, which are obviously closer to the world of work, on the analogy of the old social ranking of a leisure class above a working class, but this tiresome nonsense is now abandoned. We no longer think of leisure and work as associated with different classes, but as alternating activities within all classes, so far as we still have classes. What is relevant is that the useful arts may be well designed or badly designed, and may include or exclude ornament. Design and ornament both imply some transcendence of the world of work.

The connection with work, however, makes it clear that creative and critical energies come from human society as a whole. They give the individual a far greater importance in the work of society, but they cannot be simply 'subjective' if by subjective we mean something confined to the individual psyche. Psychology has much to say about the creative process, and psychology, though it is increasingly concerned with group therapies, still takes the individual as its main base of operations. Freud was the first to link the dream within the individual, which expresses the primary concerns of the individual, with the myths that are the main verbal culture of primitive societies and go on to form the shaping narratives of literature. But literature, even in its most mythological phases, communicates, and the dreamer cannot, without special training, understand his own dreams. Jung went a step further in identifying a collective unconscious, where we find images representing rudimentary designs of the human cosmos. But the collective unconscious is by definition still unconscious. The arts, said Plato, are dreams for awakened minds: only a collective consciousness can perform their communicating tasks.

I spoke of the sense of individual integrity as the sign of a mature society, but the isolated individual, even when equipped with a conscience and a private judgment, is essentially a sleeping animal: he can pursue his primary concerns on a physical level, but his creative and critical powers cannot extend beyond dreams. Luther did not say at Worms, 'Here I stand, because my conscience and private judgment tell me to.' He said, 'Here I stand, until I can be convinced otherwise by arguments drawn from the Word of God.' His individuality was rooted in his social and religious conditioning, growing out of them as a tree grows out of its roots; but it was not a simple expression of conditioning, or we should never have heard of him again.

The creative impulse, however central to all that is best in human life, has still much in it of what a more old-fashioned way of speaking calls 'instinctive.' It certainly employs intellectual and rational powers, but often circumvents them, working by an intuitive skill or flair that avoids explicit formulation. For many creative people consciousness would be only a self-consciousness that would block and frustrate them. Let us turn to the critical faculty. The Book of Genesis tells us that God made the world in six days and rested on the seventh, devoting six days to work and one day to the contemplation of what he had done. It adds that as this forms part of God's activity, it is a model for man to imitate. Man's consciousness of being in nature though not wholly of it is potentially a sabbatical vision, and one which includes a more leisurely and detached vision of what he is doing and why he has done it. This kind of leisurely freedom of consciousness is part of what is expressed by the word 'liberal' as applied to education.

New categories of consciousness, such as those expressed in such words as *beauty* or *ugliness* begin to arise here. To paraphrase Matthew Arnold again, many things are not seen in their full reality until they are seen, not necessarily as beautiful, but as existing within the context of beauty. Arnold was followed by Ruskin and Morris, who insisted that the reality of Victorian civilization was bound up with the sense of how much ugliness was included in it. For us too, no one who drives through the Ontario countryside can miss the reality of beauty in the woods and crop lands and running streams, or the reality of ugliness in the outskirts of towns and cities. It follows from all we have said about the priority of social to individual consciousness that such helplessly subjective formulas as 'beauty is in the eye of the beholder' will not do, however flexible such judgments may be. If there is not a consensus of some kind, we are not working with very useful conceptions.

The word *beauty* went out of fashion for a long time because it was subject to heavy ideological pressures of the wrong kind. Whether applied to Mozart's music or Monet's painting, to a nubile young woman in a bikini, or to the trees, flowers, butterflies, and sunsets that we see in nature, it tended to be associated with a sense of what was comfortable and reassuring. Entering the young woman with the bikini in a 'beauty' contest seems to imply that only young, healthy, and, very often, white, bodies can be beautiful. We may come to understand that our sense of the reality of beauty grows in proportion as we abandon this exclusive rubbish and discover beauty in more and more varieties of experience. But something of the static and established convention clings to the word. William Morris urged us to have nothing in our homes that we do not either know to be useful or believe to be beautiful. The shift in the verb is significant: as we saw earlier, belief, like beauty, often seeks the goal of reassurance rather than discovery.

I think we can use our conception of primary concern to come to a more satisfactory criterion of beauty and ugliness. These concerns, food, sex, property, and mobility, obviously have to be central in all the work we do to build a human environment out of the natural one. When the work-energy relaxes to the point at which leisure, contemplation, and critical evaluation begin to supplement it, we start thinking in terms of what in the environment is genuinely human and what is, as we say, 'dehumanizing.' What we accept as beautiful or attractive or in accord with the way we want things to be has some connection, however indirect, with the satisfying of these concerns, and what we call ugly or dehumanized – air choked with pollution, land turned into waste land by speculators, infernos created by technological idiocies from Chernobyl to Exxon Valdez – with the frustration of them. For a long time the established powers in society looked at their civilization and said, 'Probably much of it is very ugly, but that doesn't matter as long as we make profits out of it, and certainly nothing is going to be done about it.' When it becomes clear that ugly is beginning to mean dangerous as well, however, the point of view may slowly change.

The greatest of all philosophers who took criticism as his base of operations, Kant, examined three aspects of the critical faculty. First was pure reason, which contemplates the objective world within the framework of its own categories, and hence sees the objective counterpart of itself, the world as it may really be eluding the categories. Second was practical reason, where a conscious being is assumed to be a conscious will, and which penetrates farther into the kind of reality we call existential, even into experience relating to God. Third was the aesthetic faculty dealing with the environment within the categories of beauty, a critical operation involving, for Kant, questions of the kind we have just called teleological, relating to purpose and ultimate design.

For Kant, however, the formula of beauty in the natural world at least was 'purposiveness without purpose.' The crystallizing of snowflakes is beautiful because it suggests design and intention and yet eludes these things. To suggest that the design of a snowflake has been produced by a designer, whether Nature or God, suggests also that somebody or something has worked to produce it: such a suggestion limits its beauty by cutting off the sense of a spontaneous bursting into symmetry. 'Fire delights in its form,' says Blake, and Wallace Stevens adds that we trust the world only when we have no sense of a concealed creator.

The argument of Kant's *Critique of Judgment* thus turns on the close connection between aesthetic and suspended teleological judgments. This is connected with the fact mentioned earlier, that scientific explanations tend to the mechanistic and avoid the teleological. Science is concerned with parts of a whole: teleological explanations reason from the whole to the parts, and science cannot adopt this perspective unless the scientist is prepared to say that he understands the mind of God or the hidden designs of nature. What teleology we do have is surrounded by a very limited human perspective. Isaiah may imagine a state in which the lion lies down with the lamb, but we live in a state in which the lion could not exist without eating lambs, or something dietetically equivalent. If the lion had a teleology, he would say that lambs exist for the purpose of being eaten by lions; if the lamb had one, its view would be that lambs exist for the sake of being lambs, and that lions are an unwarranted and evil intrusion into their world. So naturally, when we come to the human view, we tend to assume that nature was created for man to exploit, man being the predator set in authority over all other predators.

It is clear that within the last two or three decades we have come to something of a crisis in our view of the relation both of human beings to one another and of the relation of the human to the natural environment. The questions of teleology, of the purposes and final causes of our existence, cannot be ignored much longer, even if we cannot as yet consider such questions outside the human perspective. All around us we hear demands for a society where the concerns of everybody should be recognized, where there is enough peace and freedom to enable human beings to live with full human dignity and self-respect. The Gospels suggest that the ultimate reason for wanting to live in such a world is that only in it can there be any real love. In the civilized state of humanity we love those who are close to us: for those farther away we feel the tolerance and good will which express love at a distance. In the pure state of nature we feel only possessive about those close to us, and hostile and mistrustful of those further away. The latter do all sorts of vaguely irritating things, like speaking different languages, eating different foods, and holding different beliefs.

However, the immense increase in the speed of communication today has also increased our sense of involvement with people at a distance, and even people who actually are totally alien to ourselves in their mental processes. It is difficult not to feel some involvement even with the fantasies of a psychotic murdering women who want to be engineers. One hopes that underlying the drive toward peace and freedom in our time is an impulse toward love growing out of a new immediacy of contact. The word love may still sound somewhat hazy and sentimental, but it does express some sort of crisis: 'We must love one another or die,' as W.H. Auden says.

Such love readily extends from the human to the natural world, and the feeling that nature should be cherished and fostered rather than simply exploited is one of the few welcome developments of the last generation or so. Here, again, love at a distance expresses itself as tolerance: if we can't exactly love sharks or piranhas we can still be curious about them, study their habits and leave them alone to fulfil their function in maintaining the balance of nature. The balance of nature, as these examples show, is amoral but not immoral: standards of morality are relevant only to the human world. What is immoral is humanity's inept interference with the balance of nature that has encouraged pathological developments like the Dutch elm blight or the presence of lampreys and zebra mussels in the Great Lakes.

The Redemption of Nature

To recapitulate, with the coming of consciousness humanity is sufficiently detached from nature to see it as an objective order. Apart from the efforts at survival, we are impressed with nature's size and strength and our own littleness and insignificance. This is the stage in which we find the numinous in nature, the stage that the Bible calls idolatry and that Blake regards as continuing in the mechanistic scientific outlook that he symbolizes by the name of Newton. In the next stage we realize that human values are to be found only in the human world, and that God, as distinct from the gods created by man out of nature, is to be sought for through human and social means. With words like *beauty* we begin to get some glimpse of Blake's 'threefold [vision] in soft Beulah's night.' Beulah for Blake is the earthly paradise, the state of innocence, the peaceable kingdom and married land of Isaiah 11:6 and 62:4. Beulah in Blake is much the same as the holiday world of the imagination that I identified earlier with literature and the other arts, where there is entertainment without argument. Blake describes it elsewhere as a place 'where no dispute can come.' What he meant by a fourfold vision is beyond our present scope.

There is always something of the kindergarten about garden-paradises: in Isaiah's peaceable kingdom the predatory animals converted to a new way of life are led by a child, and Adam and Eve, living in a garden planted by a benevolent parental figure, are also clearly children whose curiosity and lack of experience get them into trouble. We normally think of an earthly paradise as a world of beauty, and the word *beauty*, as we saw, has inherited some of these immature and overprotective associations. It was for this reason that the eighteenth century added the conception of 'sublime' to the conception of beauty. The sublime conveys the sense of the majestic and awful in the natural environment: that is, it preserves something of the alienation that we also feel there, but an alienation that we can find exhilarating rather than humiliating. With the present feeling for the importance of 'wet lands' and the like, we begin to understand what the poet Gerard Manley Hopkins meant by his line 'Long live the weeds and the wilderness yet' and take one more step toward envisaging a human order that has come to terms with nature on something more like nature's own terms.

We see, then, human beings continually trying to struggle out of the atavisms of tyranny and anarchy, knowing that they are better than these conditions, repeatedly forced back into them by all the perversities of their own will, yet never quite losing hope or the vision of an ideal. Such an ideal has to be present and realizable, as opposed to the dream of restoring a paradise lost in the past, or in what is symbolized by the past.

From what has been said already it is clear that this realizable ideal is the spiritual kingdom revealed by Jesus in the Gospels, which is something that only Paul's *soma pneumatikon* can even understand, much less enter. The program of spiritual awareness laid down in that tremendous philosophical masterpiece, Hegel's *Phenomenology of Spirit*, turns on two principles that are relevant here. First is Hegel's introductory principle, 'The true substance is subject.' That is, the gap between a conscious perceiving subject and a largely unconscious objective world confronts us at the beginning of experience. All progress in knowledge, in fact in consciousness itself, consists in bridging the gap and abolishing both the separated subject and the separated object.

At a certain point, for Hegel, we move from the soul-body unit, Paul's natural man, into the realm of Spirit (*Geist*: the first translation of Hegel's book into English mistranslated Geist as 'mind,' which confuses, among other things, the whole religious dimension of Hegel's argument). Spirit, says Hegel, enters the picture as soon as 'We' and 'I' begin to merge, when the individual speaks as a discriminating and independent unit within his society. In his 'substance is subject' principle Hegel continues a philosophical tradition going back to the Latin church fathers, brooding on the relation of person and substance in the Trinity and translating *hypostasis* not as *substantia* but as *persona*. The problem is to define what is at once spiritual and substantial, the spirit which is also a body. The mirror, where a subject sees an object which is both itself and not itself, is a central metaphor of knowledge, and such words as 'speculation' and 'reflection' point to its importance. Hegel is in search of a self-awareness that culminates, for him, in 'absolute knowledge,' where we finally break out of the mirror, the prison of Narcissus.

A celebrated ceramic known as the Grecian urn, which some scholars believe to have been a piece of Wedgwood pottery, informs us, in the context of an ode of Keats, that

> Beauty is truth, truth beauty: that is all
> Ye know on earth, and all ye need to know.

We have seen that a knowledge of ugliness, in both human and natural worlds, is just as essential. Again, gaining knowledge of the physical environment in the natural sciences is a pursuit of truth, even though we accept the fact that there are no permanent or final truths in science or any other human discipline. But truth always has a 'whether we like it or not' element about it, and it is difficult to separate liking or repulsion from the beauty-ugliness category. Keats saw things with an intensity that only the highest genius combined with tuberculosis can give, but here he must be speaking from a different and more idealized context.

I think Keats means that truth and beauty are both fictions, both something created by humanity out of the natural environment. One is concerned with the ordering of what is there, the other with the vision of what ideally should be there. In actual experience these two things are always different, but that is because actual experience is largely unreal. The world in which the real and the ideal become the same thing is by definition real, even if we never live in it. Truth is beauty only if the spiritual is substantial.

This understood, it is clear that the pursuit of truth in science, or anywhere else, opens up an infinite number of roads to beauty. Similarly, there may be, first, a great beauty in a literary structure which is detached but not turned away from the social and natural worlds, regardless of the content, which, because it may reflect any aspect of life, could be squalid, terrible, obscene, or insane. Second, imaginative structures contain a vast amount of truth about the human condition that it is not possible to obtain in any other way.

So Matthew Arnold's definition of literature as a criticism of life is a great deal more than a paradox. Creation includes criticism as a part of itself. For Kant, as we saw, aesthetic questions were bound up with the critical faculty of judgment. Critics have been deluded into thinking that their function is to judge works of art, but their judicial role does not go in this direction at all. They do not judge the writer, except incidentally: they work with the writer in judging the human condition. The writer may let them down: there is as much falsehood in literature as there is in any area of human utterance. To give a random example, the adoption of a 'socialist realism' program in Stalinist Russia meant that every Soviet novel had to lie from beginning to end, or its author would find himself in a concentration camp in Siberia. In other societies authors may struggle to tell the truth as they see it, but they are limited beings in a limited society, and what they say will reveal both kinds of limitation. That is why we have to have a tradition of criticism that keeps studying and commenting on the literature of the past, recognizing its relation both to its own time and to the critic's time. Out of this may come, eventually, a consensus that will broaden and deepen our understanding of our imaginative heritage.

The previous chapter drew a distinction between primary and secondary concerns, in which the secondary ones were ideological and the primary ones physical, though the physical concerns needed a spiritual dimension. This immediately raised the question of the difference between secondary concerns and spiritual primary ones. I answered this tentatively by saying that secondary concerns referred to 'primitive' societies that absorbed the individual into the group, and that the spiritual primary ones existed only in 'mature' societies that existed for the sake of individuals. We can perhaps see now that what we have been calling criticism in the larger sense as a process that takes over from the critics is the key to the distinction.

We have to have this critical approach in all the arts, and in fact in every aspect of life, so that the word criticism expands until it is practically synonymous with education itself. It covers all we know on earth and most of what we can know, if not quite, perhaps, all we need to know. In religion, too, we must keep a critical attitude that never unconditionally accepts any socially established form of revelation. Otherwise, we are back to idolatry again, this time a self-idolatry rather than an idolatry of nature, where devotion to God is replaced by the deifying of our own present understanding of God. Paul tells us that we are God's temples: if so, we should be able to see the folly of what was proposed by the Emperor Caligula for the Jerusalem temple, of putting a statue of ourselves in its holy place.

Criticism in the human world, however, is inseparably bound up with creation. We also think of God as above everything else a creator, as the opening sentence of the Bible tells us he is. I said earlier that we have abandoned the snobbish social analogy in the distinction between fine and useful (or 'minor') arts, but another distinction of some importance is involved here, in a different context. We normally say that people 'make' baskets and pots and textiles, but 'create' symphonies and dramas and frescos. Traditionally, however, we ignore this distinction when we speak of God as having 'made' the world. To call God a maker implies that divine creation is a metaphor projected from something that man does, although the Hebrew word for 'created' (*bara*) is never used in a human context. There is something denigrating to God in regarding him as a maker, as preoccupied with ingenious designs, to be complimented, as he was by natural theologians in the eighteenth century, in his cleverness in dividing up the orange into sections for convenience in (human, of course) eating. It was this consideration that led Kant to his 'purposiveness without purpose' formula for beauty. God did not make a humanly useful world; his creation relates to a world, or rather to a condition of being, that exists for its own sake, and for his. For a designing craftsman-God, a super-Hephaestus, there would have been no point in a sabbatical vision to become the model for an expanding human consciousness: only a creating God would provide a Sabbath, and with it the escape for man from natural into spiritual vision.

Chapter Three

The Double Vision of Time

Space and Time

In the first chapter I tried to distinguish spiritual language, founded on the principle that literal meaning in religion is metaphorical and mythical meaning, from natural language, which is founded on the principle that the literal is the descriptive. In the second I tried to distinguish spiritual and natural visions of the spatial world. The natural vision of space is founded on the subject-object split, and whatever is objectified in ordinary experience is 'there,' even if it is in the middle of our own backbones. At the centre of space is 'here,' but 'here' is never a point, it is always a circumference. We draw a circle around ourselves and say that 'here' is inside it. What is, in the common phrase, neither here nor there does not exist, at least in space.

As natural perception develops, the 'here' circle keeps enlarging: the very word nature, the sense of the objective as an order, shows how far we have gone in overcoming the subject-object split. In proportion as spiritual perception begins to enter the scene, we are released from the bondage of being 'subjected' to a looming and threatening objective world, whether natural or social. In the spiritual world everywhere is here, and both a centre and a circumference. The first book of philosophy that I read purely on my own and purely for pleasure was Whitehead's *Science and the Modern World*, and I can still remember the exhilaration I felt when I came to the passage: 'In a certain sense, everything is everywhere at all times. For every location involves an aspect of itself in every other location. Thus every spatio-temporal standpoint mirrors the world.' This was my initiation into what Christianity means by spiritual vision.

We saw that we have two stages to pass through, the natural and the social, before the spiritual vision of space is fully emancipated. I now want to distinguish the spiritual vision of time from the natural one, and here again we have a distinction between time in the physical world and time in the social or human world, the latter being what we call history. Philosophers have been extremely profound about time: I do not have enough philosophy to be profound, so I shall have to settle for simplicity, which in a technical subject always means being simplistic.

In our ordinary experience of time we have to grapple with three dimensions, all of them unreal: a past that is no longer, a future that is not yet, and a present that is never quite. We are dragged backwards along a continuum of experience, facing the past with the future behind us. The centre of time is 'now,' just as the centre of space is 'here,' but 'now,' like 'here,' is never a point. The first thing that the present moment does is vanish and reappear in the immediate past, where it connects with our expectation of its outcome in the future. Every present experience is therefore split between our knowledge of having had it and our future-directed fears or hopes about it. The word 'now' refers to the spread of time in between.

We know nothing of the future except by analogy with the past, and analogy tells us that we are mortal. It even seems probable that the basis of consciousness, Paul's *soma psychikon*, is the awareness that the uneasy pact between soul and body will dissolve sooner or later, whether the soul is confident that it will survive the separation or not. Meanwhile there is, coming from the bodily side, a will to survive of which the motor force is usually called desire. The continuum of desire consists largely of avoiding the consciousness of death, and acting on the assumption that we are not going to die at once. This means that our life in time is a conflict of desire and consciousness producing a state of more or less subdued anxiety, and all the higher religions begin by trying to do something about that anxiety. Buddhism tells us to extinguish desire and cut off the anxiety rooted in the past; the Gospels tell us to take no thought for the morrow and cut off the anxiety rooted in the future.

We may talk about a beginning and an end to time, but we cannot realize such things in our imaginations. Whether we speak of a creation by God which began time (that is, our experience of time) or of a big bang many billions of years ago, the human mind cannot help thinking that there must have been time 'before' that. St Augustine was bothered by this question, which he raises several times, notably in a famous passage in the *Confessions*, where in effect he answers the question, 'What was God doing before creation?' by saying, 'Preparing a hell for those who ask such a question.' If we were to guess at the repressed elements in the saint's mind when he wrote this, they might well have run something like this: If you ask God what happened before time, you embarrass God, who probably doesn't know either, and as God hates to be embarrassed, you are risking a good deal by asking.

Life in time represents the revolt of the finite against the indefinite. Time never begins or ends; life always does. Our experience of the present moment, or now, where 'now' is the spread of time between a second or two of past and future, repeats in miniature the whole sequence of our lives. Life in its turn is founded on the alternating movements in time, the cyclical patterns that give us light and darkness, summer and winter, and any number of other cyclical rhythms not yet wholly understood. The relation of life and time to language follows similar patterns. For animals, what corresponds to speech seems to have its roots in the rituals that are punctuation marks in the flow of time, and crucial points in its cycles. Thus we have mating rituals, territorial rituals, rituals of hostility to an invader, or of solidarity within a group, usually connected with communication by sound, as in the songs of birds. The same associations of speech with erotic or hostile or socially binding rituals reappear in human life. But in human rituals we have a more complex factor.

In some societies rituals may be observed on a more or less unconscious basis. If asked why such rituals, which may be very elaborate and apparently significant, are performed, such a society may have little to say to a visiting anthropologist except 'we have always done this.' But it is more usual to have some explanation of ritual at hand and to recite it as an essential part of the ritual itself. Such an explanation regularly takes the form of a myth, or story (*mythos*), recounting some event in the past of which the ritual is a commemoration or repetition, in the same way that Christmas commemorates and repeats the birth of Christ, even though we do not know the day when Christ was born. A myth in its turn is part of a mythology, or interconnected group of myths, many of them growing out of the rituals of a society's liturgical year. And, of course, the myth springs out of life, not time: it performs the same revolutionary and arbitrary act of beginning and ending.

In the Athens of the fifth century BC, a momentous step in human consciousness occurred when the rituals associated with Dionysus developed into drama, and the great evolution of what we now call literature out of mythology took a decisive turn. The specific literary genre produced on that occasion was tragedy, and tragedy, as analyzed by Aristotle, exhibits the same shape, a parabola in which 'now' is spread between a past and a future that we have been looking at, though of course on a larger scale. Oedipus, for example, is a humane and conscientious king of Thebes, whose kingdom is ravaged by a drought. The gods are angry, and it is his responsibility to find out why. He consults an oracle, the prophet Tiresias, and is told that he himself killed his father long ago and is now living in incest with his mother. Oedipus had no knowledge of this, but ignorance of the law is no excuse. So he tears out his eyes in a revulsion of horror. The knowledge that Oedipus gets from Tiresias about his own earlier life constitutes for him the moment of what Aristotle calls *anagnorisis*, which may be translated as either 'discovery' or 'recognition,' depending on whether one remembers it or not.

As a structural principle in tragedy, *anagnorisis* is a point of awareness near the end that links with the beginning, and shows us that what we have been following up to that point is not a simple continuum but something in the shape of a parabola, a story that begins, rises, turns, moves downward, and ends in catastrophe. This last word preserves the downward-turning metaphor.

This parabola shape occurs at every instant of our lives. Every experience is a recognition of having had it an instant earlier. It follows that the past is the sole source of knowledge, even though it extends up to the previous moment. The same parabola shape encompasses our entire lives. As we grow older, we find our childhood experiences becoming increasingly vivid, and the speech of old men is full of reminiscences of early life. One reason why such reminiscence is apt to be tedious is that these memories are mainly screen memories, memories not of what happened but of what they have reconstructed in their minds since. However, if they recalled what actually happened it might well be even more tedious.

The great achievement of Oedipus' life came when he encountered the sphinx and was asked the riddle, What animal crawls on four legs, then walks on two, then staggers about on three? The answer, of course, is man, who in the tragic perspective of human life is thrown blindly into the world, rises from the ground to an erect posture, then sinks slowly back toward the ground again. Some years ago an anthropologist visiting one of the South Sea islands (Malekula) found an interesting myth there. When a man dies, he meets a ferocious monster who draws half of an elaborate pattern in the sand: if the departed spirit has not been taught the other half of the pattern, and cannot complete it, the monster devours him. Similarly, what the sphinx gave Oedipus was only half of the tragic riddle of man: it was Tiresias who enabled Oedipus to complete it. Completing the pattern did not save him; it destroyed him, but Oedipus was living in this world, where completed patterns are normally tragic. Since Freud's work a century ago, we have come to understand that everyone's life repeats the Oedipal situation, and, more generally, that our character and behaviour are based on patterns formed before we can remember forming them.

Aristotle explains that a tragic action is usually set off by an overweening or aggressive act on the part of the hero, which disturbs the balance of nature, angers the gods, or provokes retaliation from other men. The aggressive act is called hubris, and the restoring of order after such aggression, which takes the form of a tragic catastrophe, is called nemesis. But long before Aristotle, the philosopher Anaximander had suggested that merely getting born is an aggressive act, a rebellion of life against time, and that death is the nemesis or restored balance that inevitably follows. Tragedy is thus a special application to life as a whole, though more striking, because the tragic hero is usually larger than life size, and his death proportionately more remarkable. Time itself seems to have no purpose except to continue indefinitely, and we are often told that it will eventually pull all life down into a heat-death in which no form of life will be able to come to birth at all. This law of entropy applies only to closed systems, and there is no certainty that the entire universe is a closed system or even that there is a universe, but the law sounds so pointlessly lugubrious that it instantly carries conviction to many people.

In the metaphorical diagrams that we always use in discussing such subjects, time inevitably has the shape of a horizontal line, the 'ever-rolling stream' that carries us along with its current. Life with its beginning and ending forms a series of parabolas, of rises and falls, along this line, following the cyclical rhythm that nature also exhibits. So far as our experience goes, the manifestations of life are always new: the eggs and rabbits of this Easter are not those of last Easter. For religions that accept the myth of reincarnation the same life may appear over and over: this doctrine does not seem to be functional in the biblical religions, though the Bible has parallel conceptions based on metaphorical identities. In Revelation 11:8, for example, Sodom, Egypt, and Jerusalem at the time of the Crucifixion are all 'spiritually' (metaphorically) the same place.

In any case, if time is metaphorically a horizontal line or

something that moves that way, is there a vertical dimension to life that a conscious mind can grasp? Most religions, certainly the biblical ones, revolve around a God who is metaphorically 'up there,' associated with the sky or upper air. In Christianity, Christ comes down from an upper region (*descendit de coelis*, as the creed says) to the surface of this earth, then disappears below it, returns to the surface in the Resurrection, then, with the Ascension, goes back into the sky again. Thus the total Christian vision of God and his relation to human life takes the metaphorical shape of a gigantic cross.

Time and History

Let us turn now from the natural context of life in time to the social and human context that we call history. Here we have, first of all, the unceasing flow of time to which society adapts in the form of what Edmund Burke calls the continuum of the dead, the living, and the unborn. It is this social continuum out of which we grow, and it is clear that an impulse toward social coherence and stability is as deeply rooted in the human consciousness as anything can be. I cannot think of any society in history that has disintegrated simply through a lack of will to survive. Consequently I do not believe what I so often hear from the news media today, that Canada is about to blunder and bungle its way out of history into oblivion, leaving only a faint echo of ridicule behind it.

Burke felt that this continuum of society was the true basis of what is called the social contract, and that to discover what a society's contract is we should look at its present structure. Much earlier, Thomas Hobbes had come up with the myth of an *original* contract in the past, one which began history as we know it. According to this, human individuals, finding life unbearable in isolation, got together to surrender authority to a leader. Of course Hobbes's individuals could never have existed except as members of previous societies, but his version of the contract has its own mythical integrity. In a state of nature man faces what is still largely unknown, and whenever man is faced with the unknown he starts projecting his fears and anxieties into it. He projects, in this case, a whole cosmos of mysterious external authority, beginning with the gods and including the laws that are usually thought of as coming to a society from an external or objective will lost in the mists of time. The next step is to see a concrete manifestation of this external authority in his own society. At the beginning of recorded history societies are dominated by rulers with gods supporting them, a fusion of spiritual and temporal authority most complete in Egypt, where the Pharaoh was an incarnation of God. The West Semitic peoples preferred to think of earthly rulers as adopted (or 'begotten,' as in Psalm 2) sons of God, but both forms of authority were present and each reinforced the other.

The vertical dimension of a God above man was thus, from the beginning, bound up with the conception of authority and a hierarchical society. In Christian metaphor God has always been a king, a sovereign, a ruler, a lord; and earthly rulers, whether spiritual or temporal, were only too ready to claim that they were the representatives of God on earth. In the course of time other conceptions proliferated: of a chain of being stretching from God at the top to chaos at the bottom, of a universe stretching from the presence of God beyond the stars to the centre of the earth, and various others. In the later eighteenth century, with the American, French, and Industrial revolutions, the assumption of the divine right of rulers and of an ascendant class to be perpetually on top of society began to be questioned. But questioning the visible aspect of external authority soon led to questioning its invisible aspect as well.

In the later nineteenth century, with the rise of Marxism and Nietzsche's proclamation of the death of God, the vertical dimension of the cosmos disappeared for many people, and only the horizontal, or historical, dimension remained. The metaphor of William James contrasting tough-minded and tender-minded people is very central to most of us: we all want to be tough-minded, capable of grappling with things as they are and not taking refuge in consoling but outworn formulas. And for many the religious dimension of existence was by definition a tender-minded attitude. But although it was common, and still is, to hear people say, 'I believe only in history,' it is not easy to see what there is in history by itself to believe in. The record of humanity from the beginning is so psychotic that it is difficult not to feel, with Joyce's Stephen Dedalus, that history is rather a nightmare from which we are trying to awake.

Marxists, for example, though always vigilant to pounce on anyone who suggests the reality of a vertical dimension of being as totally lacking in 'historicity,' are really looking for the redemption of man within history, the 'historical process' of Marxism being assumed to lead to the end of history as we have known it. Michel Foucault, in his book *The Order of Things*, studies the shift from 'classifying' systems of thought which arranged things along hierarchical and vertical patterns of authority, and which dominated culture down to the eighteenth century, to the 'causal' or historical systems that succeeded them in the nineteenth. He remarks: 'The great dream of an end to History is the utopia of causal systems of thought, just as the dream of the world's beginnings was the utopia of classifying systems of thought.' But the Marxist historical process appears to have betrayed the millions of people who have tried to live by it, and perhaps it is time to re-examine our visions of history and time.

Let us go back to our first principle. Just as when we pull a plant up by the roots the surrounding soil will cling to it, so when we examine our experience of the present moment we find it surrounded by the immediate past and future. The Bible sees the relation of God to time as an infinite extension of the same principle. The metaphors of creation and apocalypse, at the beginning and end of the Bible, mean that in the presence of God the past is still here and the future already here. The coming of Christ from a human perspective is split between a first coming in the past and a second coming in the future. The existence of the New Testament, by making this historical-prophetic event a verbal event, transfers not only the pastness of the first coming into our own present, but the futureness (there *has* to be such a word) of the second one. The vision of the future as already here is not a fatalistic vision: it means simply that we do not have to wait or die to experience it. We speak of the eternal presence of God as timeless, but once again the language fails us: we need some such word as 'timeful' to express what the King James Bible calls the fullness of time.

The movement of the biblical narrative from creation to apocalypse, though it takes place entirely within the present, is not a closed cyclical movement: it moves from a creation to a new creation. The new one is also the old one restored: it is new only to mankind, and represents not only a new but an enlarged human experience. Similarly in the Book of Job, God intervenes in the dialogue to describe to Job the past creation that Job never saw. But, once brought into Job's present experience, it becomes a new creation in which Job is no longer a mere spectator but a participant. The restoration of Job takes place in the immediate future, but it is already incorporated in the vision. Yet the future promise is an essential part of the vision, because, as Eliot says, only through time is time conquered.

Again, Ezekiel's vision of the valley of dry bones (37) was probably, in its original context, a vision of the restoration of Israel from captivity, a future event to Ezekiel. Christianity regards it as a prophecy of the resurrection begun by the resurrection of Christ, again a future event. But there is another dimension even to the Christian view, the dimension that the Book of Revelation (14:6) calls the everlasting gospel. For Paul, the Messiah was the concealed hero of the Old Testament as well as the revealed hero of the New. The prophecy includes the future but is not fixated on the future. What Ezekiel was really seeing, then, was actual resurrection, a vertical movement from a dying present into the living presence of the spiritual body. And although Jesus often speaks of his spiritual kingdom in metaphors of the future, he makes it quite clear, in the parable of the talents and elsewhere, that it is not a good idea to throw away our lives on the assumption that an 'after' life will be a better or easier one.

History is the social memory of human experience, and in writing about it we look for beginnings and ends, even though these beginnings and ends are at least partly a technical verbal device. We also impose narrative patterns, like Gibbon's 'decline and fall' for the Roman Empire or Motley's 'rise' for the Dutch Republic, to give shape to our understanding. There is thus a combination of continuity and repetition in history-writing, and the repeated or sequential themes are a mixture of fact and organizing fiction, or myth. From Virgil to Nietzsche there have been occasional visions of history as totally cyclical, an unending movement of time in which the same events recur indefinitely. There seems to be better evidence, however, that time is irreversible, and general cyclical views of history are not convincing. That there are cyclical elements in history, that is, recurring patterns that exist in events themselves and are not simply fictions in the mind of the historian, seems inescapable.

A very frequent primitive view of history is that it consists of a series of re-enactments in time of certain archetypal myths that happened before human life as we know it began. In some societies this dominance of repetition over history is so powerful that in a sense nothing ever happens. In the Egyptian Old Kingdom a Pharaoh may set up a stele recording his defeat of his enemies, with the enemies, even their leaders, carefully named. It seems like a genuine historical record – until scholars discover that it has been copied verbatim from another monument two centuries older. What is important is not that the Pharaoh won, but that he continues to say that he won, in a ritual pseudo-history where no defeat ever can occur. This obliterating of history is much the same as the incessant rewriting of history in totalitarian states, which turns history into a continuous record of the infallibility of the ruling party.

Sometimes this sense of repetition develops a movement to create a new kind of history by reincarnating a myth out of the past. The patron saint of all such efforts is Don Quixote, who tried to force the society around him to conform to a lost age of chivalry. We note in passing that no previous age thus invoked ever existed: quixotic versions of history are secular parodies of the Christian view of the Fall, and, as Proust says, the only paradises are those we have lost. The Nazi movement in

Germany purported to be a re-creation of a mythical heroic Germany, though it soon became clear that what the Nazis were interested in re-creating were infantile sadistic fantasies. The reason is obvious: infantile fantasy is all that really presents itself to the quixotic mind. Even the garden of Eden, as we saw, was really a place of immortal childhood.

Karl Marx had something similar in view when he spoke of events occurring first as tragedy and secondly as farce. He was thinking, among other things, of the French Second Empire, where Napoleon III became emperor simply because his name was Napoleon. It is true that the end of the Third Reich was not worthy of the name of tragedy, and was more accurately a hideous farce, though a farce that only the devil would find amusing. Other attempts to live in a myth abstracted from history, such as the nineteenth-century Utopian communities in America and the Quebec separatism inspired by the motto *je me souviens*, are closer to the skewed pathos of Quixote himself.

There is a corresponding fixation on the future. In Christianity this usually takes the form of a fearful expectation of a second coming or simply a postponing of spiritual life, of the 'some day we'll understand' type, the assumption that death automatically brings enlightenment. Secular parodies of this take the form of beliefs in revolution or progress, and in their demonic form employ the tactic of sacrificing the present to the future. Such visions can be quite as horrible in their results as in their fascist counterparts. It seemed logical in Stalin's Russia that if hundreds of thousands of kulaks were murdered or sent to concentration camps right away, Russia might have a more efficient system of collectivized agriculture within the next century. But such means adopted for theoretically reasonable ends never serve such ends: they merely replace them, and the original ends disappear. All that the murdering and persecuting of kulaks accomplished, in short, was the murdering and persecuting of kulaks. The operation was not simply evil, it was unutterably futile, for in far less than a century the Soviet Union realized that it needed kulaks again. There is no reason to feel complacent about Stalin's Russia, however: many Canadians defend the destruction of their country by such phrases as 'you can't stop progress,' unaware that 'progress' in such contexts is an idol on the same level as the legendary Hindu Juggernaut or the Old Testament Moloch.

Time and Education

Hitler and Stalin between them are sufficient commentary on an attitude to time and history that becomes obsessed by its relation either to the past or to the future. We saw also that there is an element of repetition in time, in life, and in history. Let us look at this element of repetition in human experience. There are two kinds of repetition: one is inorganic, a matter of merely doing the same thing over and over; the other is habit or practice repetition that leads to the acquiring of a skill, like practising a sport or a musical instrument. Inorganic repetition is precisely what the word superstition means: binding oneself to a continuing process that is mere compulsiveness, often accompanied by a vague fear that something terrible will happen if we stop. The acquiring of a skill transforms mere repetition into something that develops and progresses. If we ask what it develops into or progresses toward, we may provisionally say something like an enlargement of freedom: we practice the piano to set ourselves free to play it. In any case, this kind of directed repetition is constantly turning into larger and more complex forms of itself: it seems even to be reduplicating the process of life, where embryo turns into infant and infant into adult.

Acquiring a skill in human life is possible, so far as we can see, only for the individual. But the social basis of individual life may provide, in its institutions, a continuity, a sense of stable and relatively predictable movement in time, on which the individual can build his directed repetition. The Church, with its sacramental system and its constant proclaiming of its gospel, exhibits a continuity of this type: so does law, with its dialectic of precedents, and so does education, so far as education presents the repeating elements of knowledge from the alphabet and multiplication table onward. It may seem strange to speak of living a religious life in terms of acquiring a skill by practice, but there is a parallel: the New Testament writers constantly use such phrases as 'without ceasing' when exhorting us to continue the practice of prayer or charity.

When the Preacher said that there was nothing new under the sun, he was speaking of knowledge, which exists only in the past, and where nothing is unique. The passing of experience into knowledge is closely related to the tragic vision of life. It is part of a reality in which at every instant the still possible turns into the fixed and unalterable past. We feel partly released from this tragic vision when we are acquiring skills, getting an education, or advancing in a religious life: there we are exploiting our memory of the past to give direction along the present. Consequently the Preacher also said, 'To every thing there is a season.' Here he was speaking of experience, where everything is unique and everything is diversified. What he means by wisdom is a double movement: it starts with present experience disappearing into past knowledge, but then reverses itself and becomes past knowledge permeating and irradiating present experience. What sounds at first like pessimistic melancholy turns into something very different as he goes on and begins to say things like 'Go thy way, eat thy bread with joy, and drink thy wine with a merry heart.' Wisdom for him is a force moving against the normal flow of time, going from the 'vanity' or emptiness of the past into the fullness of the present, and the process is a constant liberation of energy.

Thus the tragic aspect of time in which every moment brings us toward death, and in which we know only what has been, and never what is or is going to be, is counteracted by the directed and progressive attack on time that underlies all genuine achievement in everything that matters, in religion, in education, in culture most obviously. This building up of habit through incessant practice creates a new vertical dimension in experience, though it grows from the bottom upward and through the individual, however much the individual may depend on a social consensus in church or university. This vertical dimension is once again a hierarchy and a structure of authority, but these words no longer relate to temporal authority or to the supporting social structure. No human being or human institution is fit to be trusted with any temporal authority that is not subject to cancellation by some other authority. Spiritual authority, which is alone real, inheres in such things as the classic in literature, the repeatable experiment in science, or the example of the dedicated spiritual life; it is an authority that expands and does not limit the dignity of those who accept it. All personal authority in the spiritual world is self-liquidating: it is the authority of the teachers who want their students to become their scholarly equals, of the preachers who, like Moses (Numbers 11:29), wish that all God's people were prophets.

The hierarchy I spoke of begins with the bottom layer of the human psyche, or what is called the unconscious, a chaos of energy quieted and ordered by the repetition of practice. A pianist may come through practice to play thousands of notes in a few moments without consciously attending to each one. But there is of course a consciousness attending all the same, the faculty I have linked to criticism, which does not stop simply with self-criticism, but goes on to a conscious awareness of the historical context of what one is doing. The functionaries of churches and schools and courts, when they become entrenched bureaucracies, may at any time retreat into superstition, simply handing on what has been handed to them. Criticism is one of the forces that can strike a new energy out of a dormant one: it approaches the past in a way that relates it to contemporary life and concerns. Works of literature, music, and the other arts do not, apparently, improve or progress with time, but the understanding of their meaning, their importance, and their function in history can and to some extent does improve. In Christianity, while we do not think of revelation itself as progressing, the human response to it clearly can progress. In the sciences criticism is even more deeply rooted. In science every new discovery attaches itself to the total body of what is already known, so that with every major advance the whole of knowledge is created anew.

When one is a beginner, this attempt at reversing the flow of time by progressive achievement is attracted toward a future goal, the goal of mastery of the skill. But at a certain point the future is already here, the sense of endless plugging and slugging is less oppressive, and the goal is now an enlarged sense of the present moment. One has glimpses of the immense foreshortening of time that can take place in the world of the spirit; we may speak of 'inspiration,' a word that can hardly mean anything except the coming or breaking through of the spirit from a world beyond time. One may, as I have done myself, spend the better part of seventy-eight years writing out the implications of insights that have taken up considerably less than an hour of all those years. Here the shadow that falls between the present moment and the knowledge that one has lived through the present moment has disappeared, and experience and the awareness of experience have become, for an instant at least, the same thing. When this happens in a Christian context, we may say that the human spirit has found its identity with the spirit of God, and ought to know now, even from the split second of insight it has had, what is meant by resurrection and deliverance from death and hell.

For about two decades in this century a vogue for Oriental techniques of meditation, Indian yoga, Chinese Tao, Japanese Zen, swept over North America. The genuine teachers of these techniques stressed the arduous practice that was essential to them, and pointed out the futility of trying to avoid the work involved by taking lysergic acid and the like. The goal was enlightenment, the uniting of experience and consciousness just mentioned. There was some gullibility and groupie mentality in these cults, especially among those who were ready to believe anything that was Oriental and nothing that was Western. For them such words as *samadhi* and *satori*, as they had not read the New Testament, did not connect with such conceptions as 'born of the spirit,' 'fullness of time,' or the sudden critical widening of the present moment expressed by the word *kairos*. But some analogies may have come through by osmosis.

For example, the Oriental scriptures tell us that very advanced stages of enlightenment bring miraculous powers of various kinds, including healing, but that these powers should never be regarded as more than incidental by-products, and may even distract one from the real goal of liberation. If so, the miraculous element in the Gospels, which describe a life lived on a plane of intensity that none of us have much conception of, should cause no surprise, and there are clear indications that the gospel writers were more impressed by Jesus' miracles than Jesus himself was. Jesus performs his miracles with reluctance, almost with irritation; he imposes secrecy on those he cures; he tells his disciples that they can do as well as that themselves. But the Oriental analogues may begin to give us some faint notion of what *Heilsgeschichte* or sacred history really talks about.

I mention these cults because they seem to me to be an aspect, even if a minor one, of a general weariness with history, with being bullied and badgered by all the pan-historical fantasies of the nineteenth century, of Hegel and Marx and Newman and Comte, who keep insisting that by history alone can we be saved, or rather by putting some kind of construct on history that will give it a specious direction or meaning. Even the arts may sometimes give an impression of wearing out their historical possibilities. The most profoundly original artist still forms part of a larger process of cultural aging: the music of Beethoven could only have come later than Haydn and Mozart and earlier than Wagner and Berlioz. And while we are not likely to tire of Beethoven, the cultural tradition he belongs to may reach a point of exhaustion where it becomes oppressive to carry it on without a major change.

I sometimes feel that we may be in such a period of doldrums now, with so many artists in all fields circling around over-explored conventions of literary irony or pictorial abstraction or architectural conventions that have produced the loveless and unloved erections contemplated by Prince Charles. However grateful we may be for the many writers and painters and builders we have who are so much better than that, I sense a longing for some kind of immense creative renovation, which, I should imagine, would have to be the product of a large-scale social movement. Earlier in the century a proposal for such an awakening would automatically have been responded to with the word 'revolution,' a donkey's carrot still held before the student rebels of the sixties. Revolutions, however, are culturally sterile: they weaken the traditions of the past but put nothing in their place except second-rate versions of the same thing. I think the real longing is not for a mass movement sweeping up individual concerns, but for an individualized movement reaching out to social concerns. Primary concerns, that is: food, shelter, the greening of the earth, and their spiritual aspects of freedom and equal rights.

The provision in the Mosaic code for a jubilee year showed a profound insight into the psychology of human beings living in time. I said earlier that cyclical visions of history lack convincingness, but that cyclical elements in history clearly do exist. One of these is the one so heavily featured in the Bible, the cycle of bondage and release, the cyclical oppression and restoration of Israel. We celebrate the Resurrection every Easter, but Easter by itself does not suggest resurrection; it suggests only the renewing of the cycle of time, the euphoria with which we greet the end of winter and the coming of spring. There is a similar euphoria in society when a tyranny comes crashing down and proclamations of freedom and equality are voiced on all sides. We heard this euphoria a few years ago in Haiti and in the Philippines; we are hearing it now in Eastern Europe. But we cannot trust its permanence; far less can we trust the effect produced by it on us. There are people trying to get rid of an unworkable economy with its unworking bureaucracy and there are neo-Nazi skinheads; there are crowds demonstrating for freedom and crowds demonstrating against minorities; there are revivals of free discussion and revivals of anti-Semitism. One hopes for a society that can remember on Tuesday what it thought it wanted so desperately on Monday, but on the human plane even the pressure of primary concerns, food and shelter and freedom to move and talk, cannot always be relied on to preserve such a memory. As Coleridge said, 'I could weep for the criminal patience of humanity!' Perhaps the most effective help may come from the mammon of unrighteousness: from greed and self-interest and xenophobia and the conflicts they bring with them, when harnessed against their will to better causes.

I have not spoken of the providence of God, because it seems to me that the providence of God operates only in its own sphere, not in the sphere of human folly and frivolousness. I think immense changes could be brought about by a Christianity that was no longer a ghost with the chains of a foul historical record of cruelty clanking behind it, that was no longer crippled by notions of heresy, infallibility, or exclusiveness of a kind that should be totally renounced and not rationalized to the slightest degree. Such a Christianity might represent the age of the Spirit that the thirteenth-century Franciscan Joachim of Floris saw as superseding the Old Testament age of the Father and the New Testament age of the Logos. Such a Christianity would be neither an inglorious rearguard action nor a revolutionary movement creating suffering and death instead of life more abundantly. It would be a Christianity of a Father who is not a metaphor of male supremacy but the intelligible source of our being; of a Son who is not a teacher of platitudes but a Word who has overcome the world; and of a Spirit who speaks with all the tongues of men and angels and still speaks with charity. The Spirit of creation who brought life out of chaos brought death out of it too, for death is all that makes sense of life in time. The Spirit that broods on the chaos of our psyches brings to birth a body that is in time and history but not enclosed by them, and is in death only because it is in the midst of life as well.

Chapter Four

The Double Vision
of God

Gods and God

In the three previous chapters I have been trying to suggest
something of the contrast between the natural or physical and
the spiritual vision in regard to language, space, and time. We
can now try to see where this takes us in our efforts to distinguish the natural from the spiritual vision of God. We are told
in the New Testament that God is spirit, that Jesus has no
kingdom except a spiritual one, and that only the spirit can
understand what the New Testament is saying. On the other
hand, no God or numinous presence can be found within
nature, the attempt to find him there being the great error that
the Bible calls idolatry. The metaphorical vision may see the
reflection of God from his works in nature, but it is only through
the distinctively human elements in the world that we can come
to the spiritual God.

Let us begin by looking at some features of the development
of 'pagan' or 'heathen' religion in countries outside the Bible but
contemporary with it. For human societies organized in small
tribal units, dependent on nature rather than masters of it, the
gods take shape as projections of human hopes and anxieties
into the more mysterious aspects of nature. Local deities of
rivers, trees, mountains, along with the sun and moon, are
among the most primitive of divinities and develop into the
nymphs and fauns and satyrs of later mythology. The cult of

animals that we find in Egypt and elsewhere also reflects a sense of something numinous in modes of being quite different from the human consciousness. Such a cult is not a 'worship of animals,' but a recognition that humanity is only one presence among others in its world. The sense of the numinous in nature is the bedrock of the pagan or heathen religion, which is based first on tribal and local societies, then on rural and non-urbanized parts of civilization. A pagan is etymologically a peasant (*paganus*), and a heathen a heath-dweller.

Although there is unlikely to be any clear-cut sequence, as societies form bigger units and become more elaborately class-structured, the gods take on the features of a human aristocracy. The more important gods often dwell on mountain-tops like the Greek Olympus, and dispense a rough justice like a human aristocracy, sometimes benevolent, sometimes tyrannical, but above all concerned with preserving their privileges and inflicting vicious punishments on anyone who challenges their authority, even by a boast. By that time there are many gods of primarily political and social reference, gods of war, of wisdom, and of justice, but they still reflect the arbitrary and whimsical elements in both human and physical nature.

As nations expand into empires, and their rulers begin to think of themselves as kings of the world, a supreme god appears, and religion approaches the great divide between the gods of nature who are human creations and a god who is supreme over both human and physical nature. An imperial monotheism, in which the ruler of a world-empire is the incarnation or adopted son of God, as mentioned previously, is a very different thing from the revolutionary and still largely tribal monotheism of the Bible; but still it is monotheism, and it marks an immense advance in the human comprehension of the environment. First, such monotheism is relatively tolerant: it may even encourage local cults, on a general assumption that smaller gods are emanations or reflections of the supreme one. When the Mesopotamian empires that held their conquests only by force were superseded by the better organized Persian Empire under Cyrus, the benefits for the Jews held captive in

Babylonia were immediately marked. The Roman Empire, too, was tolerant of a plurality of cults to a remarkable degree.

The physical image that suggests monotheism is usually the sky, the superior world that is above us everywhere. Some students of mythology think that most primitive communities have some potential monotheism in which a supreme god is there, but has abdicated and left the rule of the world to lesser spirits. Such a conception reflects a human society confined to small competitive groups, unable to unite even by force. Of the objects in the sky, the sun alone seems to have an obvious and immediate relevance to human concerns, and hence the ruler-figure in imperial monotheism is often associated with the sun. This association has persisted from ancient Egypt to contemporary Japan, and enters Christendom with the 'Sun King' Louis XIV of France.

Then again, monotheism of any kind indicates an increase in the human mastery of nature, both intellectual and physical. The sense of the unity of God forms part of a growing sense of nature as an order: in fact this sense goes so far as to reverse our initial statement about nature as the source of idolatry. There is a strong philosophical tradition, stretching from the Stoics to Spinoza and beyond, of identifying God and nature, though this 'nature' is no longer a world of mysterious presences but is conceived as an order obeying certain laws. Such a nature is less alien to humanity and more of a reflection of human consciousness. Of course in an originally polytheistic religion the gods do not give up at once: they are still there, if increasingly vestigial, in pagan Rome up to Julian the Apostate. Yet as early as the *Iliad* we have in the foreground a group of quarrelling gods, some lobbying for Greeks and some for Trojans, and in the background a hint that, as the fifth line of the poem tells us, a single divine purpose (Zeus) is working its will. Even that will appears sometimes to be overruled by a fate which is impersonal, and which even the greatest of personal gods must obey.

The sense of a natural order grows along with the sense of a moral order. From Plato onward there is an increasing feeling that whimsical, arbitrary, capricious gods are too human to be really divine. Our notions of the best human behaviour ought surely to be the place where our conceptions of divine behaviour should start, or, as Plutarch says, gods of whom indecent stories can be told cannot be real gods. He is thinking of such stories as the one in the *Odyssey* of the lovers Ares and Aphrodite caught in a net constructed by Hephaistos (who at the time was Aphrodite's husband), to the great amusement of the other gods.

Such developments are obviously important for religion: they also accompany the gradual transformation of mythology into literature. The theory called euhemerism, where gods are thought to be deified human heroes, is an inadequate theory for mythology, because such deification appears to be the exception rather than the rule. But the reverse process is a very real one: gods modulate into human heroes of saga and romance, and so initiate the development of secular literature, or the original myths may be thought of and retold as essentially literary stories, as they are in Ovid's *Metamorphoses*. After the coming of Christianity, Jupiter and Venus become purely literary figures, but are much more genuinely real as gods than they were when temples and sacrifices were connected with them. The true gods thus become more like what the Greeks called Muses, symbols of the creative powers of humanity, like the Eros who appears to Dante in the *Vita Nuova*, and says to him *'ego dominus tuus'*: I am thy Lord. False gods, in the Christian period, are those regarded as objective existences independent of human imagination: as no such gods exist, they can only be illusions thrown up by the demonic powers. We notice a cosmos of three levels here, a point we shall return to: the genuinely divine, the demonic parody, and the human world in between that is turned by grace from a demonic direction toward a divine one.

We have not forgotten that monotheism of the kind discussed here is imperial, and that the human being at the top of the social structure is its personal focus, becoming increasingly so as the other elements of religion become more impersonal. In Egypt the Pharaoh was an incarnation of two gods, of Horus during his life and of Osiris after his death. Obviously the deifying of a human ruler is a powerful political instrument, and one that was adopted in the Roman Empire in a ritual following the emperor's death. This device was effective enough for Augustus, but something of a strain when the emperor was one of the contemptible creatures who followed Augustus. The philosopher Seneca wrote a satire in which he described the deifying of the Emperor Claudius as an 'apocolocyntosis,' the apotheosis of a pumpkin. Still, the need for a personal focus kept the absurd custom going, and the resistance of Jews and Christians to participating in it turned them into political criminals.

Later centuries were fascinated by the contrast between the temporal ruler of the world, Augustus Caesar, and its spiritual ruler Jesus, who was born during Augustus' reign. Contemporary with Jesus we have the whole mythological side of classical culture summed up in two great masterworks, Virgil's *Aeneid* and Ovid's *Metamorphoses*. Ovid provides a kind of encyclopaedia of mythology in which the central theme is metamorphosis, the incessant dissolving and reshaping of forms of life. Toward the end of his long poem, he brings in the philosopher Pythagoras to expound a gloomy philosophy based on the same theme. The *Metamorphoses* starts with creation and deluge myths, and Pythagoras sees at the end of time a running down of the world into a kind of entropy, or chaos come again. But there are also eulogies of the Caesars, particularly Julius, as the only symbols of what can transcend metamorphosis. In Virgil, similarly, the myth that Rome was founded by Trojan refugees expands into a vision of history in which the Roman empire represents a kind of goal or *telos* of the historical process.

There is a certain amount of Stoicism behind Virgil, and Stoicism was a philosophy, or religion, that originally put its main emphasis on equality and the brotherhood of man, and had no place for a dictatorial ruler. But the logic of a revolutionary situation, which elevated the emperor to the top of the social pyramid, compelled Stoicism to adapt itself to becoming an intellectual support for the empire. Stoic and emperor, of course, merged in the figure of Marcus Aurelius. There are some odd parallels with the Marxist developments in our day: first the vision of equality in Marx himself, where the state eventually withers away, then the adulation of Lenin as the power-figure who consolidated the revolution with himself as leader, then a series of tyrants.

There are thus two foci of non-biblical religion, the ruler vested with supreme authority and the sense of nature as an impersonal structure of law and order. The ruler manifests this order in human society, and is therefore symbolically divine. Similarly, there may be a supreme personal god in Zeus for the Stoic poets, but Zeus owes his personal dignity to his impersonal aspect as a manifestation of law. The principle involved here is that religion tends to outgrow the notion of a personal god in order to reach its loftiest ideals. Or, to put it another way, we can build a higher tower of Babel with a god so transcendent that he transcends first personality and then himself, eventually disappearing beyond the bounds of human categories of thought. Even in Plotinus, who retains a personal god, that god is so remote that language cannot say what he is except 'one.' Then we come down through an immense ladder of Word, Spirit, ideas, demons and the like to something approaching the (ugh) physical world we live in. Such constructs reflect the pyramid of authority, nevertheless, in that very world.

The temporal ruler is the chief executive officer of nature, history, and God. There are two kinds of such rulers, the *tyrannos*, whose power springs from his natural abilities as a leader, and the *basileus*, who rules by hereditary right. (*Basileus* does not invariably mean a hereditary ruler, but I need some word.) Cromwell, Napoleon, Lenin were forces of nature; hereditary monarchs are attached to a social contract. The latter stand for continuity as the *tyrannos* does for revolutionary upheaval.

We think of God as the author of our being, and hence use the metaphor of 'Father' for him. If we think of the authors of our being in a natural context, we think of our parents, then of our direct ancestors. The association of divinity and nature underlies the tendency in society to produce an aristocracy, a class considered entitled to special privileges because their direct ancestors possessed them. At their head is the king, who is king because his father was a king. Such continuity is a conservative social force: once it is broken by a revolution, the *tyrannos* or natural force appears again. As Marvell says of Cromwell's ousting of Charles I:

> Nature that hateth emptiness
> Allows of penetration less,
>   And therefore must make room
>   When greater spirits come.

Hebraic and Hellenic Traditions

Christianity is founded on the New Testament, and the New Testament is founded on the Old Testament only. The New Testament is unintelligible until it is understood that its writers regarded their message as primarily an interpretation of the true meaning of the Old Testament, the spiritual fulfilment of its laws and prophecies. Nevertheless there were many in the early Christian period who thought that the break between Judaism and Christianity did not go far enough. Many of the Gnostics regarded the Jehovah of the Old Testament as an evil demiurge, and the work of Jesus as an effort to deliver humanity from his tyranny. This position was close to that of the Manicheans, who, like the second-coming sects of the previous century, were anxious to hasten the apocalypse, to jump out of matter into spirit by abstaining from sexual intercourse and the like. For the central tradition of Christianity, spirit and nature could not be instantly divorced in this way, and the Incarnation implied that the same God presides over both spiritual and natural worlds.

So Christianity retained the conception of the integrity of the Bible and of the positive relevance of the Old Testament to the New. When Augustine denounces the errors of the Manicheans, their negative attitude to the Old Testament is frequently cited. At the same time there was increasingly a search for philosophical principles to serve as an infrastructure for the biblical revelation, and to form the necessary link between the two orders. As all our philosophical traditions in the West are Hellenic in origin, this meant constructs derived ultimately from Plato or Aristotle.

There were several intellectual traditions in the Middle Ages that were Neoplatonic in their main inspiration: one of them was introduced by Dionysius the Areopagite, although he would probably have got nowhere if he had not given himself a fraudulent name out of the New Testament. It was a more concrete Aristotelian tradition, with its greater reliance on form and language, that finally prevailed with the great Summas of St Thomas Aquinas. One difficulty here is that every philosophical construct is bound to be a differentiation from every other such construct, and this cannot be fully recognized in societies preoccupied with a uniform ideology. As in all repressive cultures, most of the more penetrating thinkers of the Middle Ages were dissidents accused or at least suspected of heresy: they included Siger of Brabant, Scotus Erigena, Peter Abelard, John Wyclif, Roger Bacon, Nicholas of Autrecourt, Meister Eckhart, William of Occam, and Joachim of Floris. Dante got one or two of these into Paradise, and his own *De Monarchia* on the Index. With the Lutheran and Calvinist movements there came a renewed emphasis on the Old Testament as the sole basis for Christian doctrine, and something close to an abandoning of all attempts at an integrated philosophical infrastructure. In the Middle Ages, St Thomas was the greatest Catholic theologian, and therefore its greatest philosopher. In the sixteenth century, Luther and Calvin were the greatest Reformed theologians, and were therefore not philosophers at all.

The funeral service speaks of Christianity as providing the comfort of a reasonable religion. It is not always understood that the reasonable and the rational are opposed attitudes, and that the comfort of a reasonable religion can hardly coexist with the prickly discomfort of a rational one. The reasonable person proceeds by compromise, halfway measures, illogical agreements, and similar signs of mature human intelligence. Rationalism is a militant use of language designed to demonstrate the exclusive truth of what it works on and with. Inferior grades of rationalism usually amount to a simple defence of intolerance and obscurantism by a trumpery show of pseudo-logic, an abuse of language that succeeds only in articulating original sin. For the Reformation it would have been reasonable to have developed an interest in Judaism as the *fons et origo* of Christianity, and in the way that Jews read their own Bible. There were marginal improvements in the attitude toward Jews: a progress in the study of Hebrew through the sixteenth century and later, which depended on Jewish teachers; a slightly greater degree of social tolerance in seventeenth-century Holland (Rembrandt is sometimes thought to have been Jewish), and, after Cromwell, in England; there was even a Christian form of Kabbalism, which turned mainly on putting the letter *shin* in the middle of the Hebrew YHWH and thereby changing Yahweh to Yeshua. But it was centuries before there was any serious Christian interest in Jewish culture. Matthew Arnold's dialectic of Hellenic and Hebraic influences on the culture of nineteenth-century Britain, in *Culture and Anarchy*, is vitiated by the fact that the Hebraic was not really an influence from a different culture, but a narcissistic kidnapping of an originally Hebrew book into the reader's own cultural orbit.

There was, however, a genuine clarification of the Christian revelation involved in the renewed emphasis on the Bible, and I have often reverted to a passage in Milton's *Paradise Regained* (IV, 285ff) that illustrates what it is. In that poem, which deals with the temptation in the wilderness, Satan first tries to persuade Christ to join the Parthians and become a kind of Genghis Khan, then to become emperor of Rome and achieve temporal power over the world. Failing in these, he goes on to suggest that Jesus attach himself to the Hellenic philosophical tradition. Jesus denies that there is any relevance to his own Messianic function in the Greek tradition, and refuses to have anything to do with any culture outside the Old Testament. The passage is often regarded as evidence of a tired, irritable, even sick reaction on Milton's part; but in its context what Jesus says makes complete sense. The world, including the wisdom of Plato and Aristotle, is in Satan's possession: Jesus must reject every atom of it before he can enter on his ministry. After he has done that, he can redeem everything in that world that is not inseparably attached to the demonic, including Hellenic culture. It is only because Christ rejects Plato and Aristotle that Milton himself can study them.

The conception of redemption is a centrally Christian element in contrast to, for example, the more simplistic Manicheanism, where there are only the divine and demonic worlds, and those elected for salvation are not so much redeemed as rescued. A man rescued from a shipwreck is simply pulled out of the water, and wants to have nothing more to do with water; but redemption means fulfilling what one formerly was, as well as separating it from the demonic or parody-world of evil. A redeemed slave has his bondage annihilated, but his essential human life fulfilled; similarly with the Old Testament law as the New Testament conceives of it, which is fulfilled in one aspect and abolished in another.

Thus the immense benefits of Hellenic culture for the Western tradition, including Christianity, are not in question here: the question is the emphasis on Hellenic philosophical conceptions rather than the Old Testament as the basis of Christian teachings. The growth of democratic ideology increasingly compelled Christianity to be reasonable, to soft-pedal its claims to being the exclusive means of human redemption, and not simply to tolerate but to enter into dialogue with other religions or anti-religions. But in all centuries there is a perpetually renewed hankering for a rational infrastructure that will demonstrate the unique validity of the Christian revelation once and for all. In the twentieth century this tendency produced, two generations ago, a revived Thomism in Catholic thought, set up to be a comprehensive intellectual system in opposition to Marxism. In Protestant circles, Harnack audibly wished that Christianity had been based on classical rather than Hebraic sources. Matthew Arnold, with many qualifications, would probably have agreed. Such revisionism would doubtless not have translated the 'Logos' in the Gospel of John as 'Word,' but would rather have tried to assimilate it to the philosophical Logos in Greek thought from Heraclitus onward, where it is more like a principle of order in the mind that recognizes a corresponding order in the physical world. Most Protestantism, however, turned to history rather than metaphysics as an infrastructure for revelation. We have already glanced at the method resulting: we first distinguish secular from sacred history, then ignore the mythical structure of sacred history in favour of extracting a credible historical Jesus of secular history from the wrong context.

Paul could explain to the legalistic Romans that Christ was the fulfilment of the law, and to the erotic Corinthians that Christ was the fulfilment of love. Perhaps if he had succeeded in founding a church at Athens he would have written an Epistle to the Athenians that would have clarified something of the Hebraic-Hellenic relationship. He shows a token interest in Hellenistic culture, at least, in quoting Menander and the Stoic poet Aratus of Solis (I Corinthians 15:33; Acts 17:28). In default of such an epistle, the only reasonable thing to do is to return to our principle that the language of both testaments is the language of myth and metaphor.

Metaphorical Literalism

The general position we start from is, once again, that the true literal sense of the Bible is metaphorical. This conception of a metaphorical literal sense is not new, or even modern. Dante said that his *Commedia* was, like Scripture itself, 'polysemous,' having many meanings, though in his exposition the literal-descriptive is the basis of all meaning. He passes over the immense difficulties involved in explaining how a poem could have this kind of literal meaning, and one of his first commentators, his son Pietro, remarks that there are in fact different kinds of literal meaning, of which the metaphorical literal is one. But this insight remained undeveloped in biblical criticism because of official anxieties about dispensing with the simplistic literal.

In Matthew and Luke, genealogies of Jesus are given to show that he was legitimately descended from David as the Messiah was supposed to be by prophecy. It is hard to see just what these genealogies establish: apart from the fact that the two lists are quite different for the post-exilic period, they both trace the descent through Joseph, who according to the Virgin Birth story was not Jesus' father at all. Besides, while Jesus was a Jew, descended from Abraham like all Jews, we are told (Matthew 3:9) that the Jews need not pride themselves on that descent, as God could raise up more descendants of Abraham from stones (an image curiously similar to the story of Deucalion and Pyrrha in Ovid's flood myth). As for the Virgin Birth, it looks like an importing of the common Mediterranean myth of the hero with a divine father and a human mother, complete with the need for concealing the miraculous birth from the person threatened by it, in this case Herod. The most likely reason for importing it appears to be the Septuagint rendering of *halma*, young woman, as virgin, *parthenos*, in Isaiah 7:14.

This kind of disintegration is as far as we can get with what Blake calls single vision. But the real literal question is not 'Did this happen just like that?' but 'Is this an essential part of the revelation of the Messiah?' If we look back at what we said about *basileus* and *tyrannos* authority-figures in secular life, we can see that the story of the Messiah must include the *basileus* theme of Davidic descent, but that in the double vision which includes the spiritual one, it is equally necessary that the hereditary succession should be interrupted by a divine intervention. Otherwise we should be ascribing divine right to the natural father or direct ancestor, as human monarchies do. The line of David itself was established by divine intervention, though Saul remained the Lord's anointed after his rejection. The Virgin Birth, where God raises up a son of David, not out of a stone but certainly without a natural father, is essential to understanding what the real or spiritual significance of Jesus is.

Jesus is a spiritual *basileus*, a legitimate king, totally unrecognized as such in a historical context, except in mockery, but invariably addressed as 'Lord' by his followers. He is also a spiritual *tyrannos*, owing his unique abilities as leader not to nature or fate or the historical process, but directly to the will of

God. In contrast, Augustus, the temporal ruler of the world when Jesus was born, is a potential Antichrist figure, that is, a human ruler who claims divine honours, and he became an actual Antichrist, as mentioned earlier, when deified by the Roman cult.

We note that the principle of metaphorical literalism takes its chances with the possibility that the Gospels are cleverly concocted pious frauds. If the gospel writers had simply made up what they say out of their own imaginations or even out of their convictions, what they produced would still have been superb works of literature, though they would not have been the Gospels. A superb work of literature is a very precious thing in a literary context, and to the extent that this context is involved, the Gospels are authentic literary treasures. Approaching the Gospels as one would approach works of literature, however, though a correct approach on the literal level, is confined to that level. The Bible is still polysemous, and has many other dimensions of meaning beyond the suspended judgment of the imaginative. Some of them would recapture everything that the single-vision literalist is trying to gain, but an exclusive single-vision literalism will not work.

In *Twelfth Night*, when Viola and Sebastian appear together, the Duke says, 'A natural perspective, that is and is not!' The phrase 'natural perspective' refers to the fact that in ordinary experience it is impossible that even twins could be so much alike, but this is a play, and in a play we may have visual confirmation of what otherwise would be only the metaphor of 'identical' twins. In Mark 1:6, John the Baptist is described as wearing camel-hair clothes and a leather girdle. Ah, says the single-vision reader, at last a realistic detail. There are no realistic details in the Gospels: this detail is there to identify John with the Elijah of II Kings 1:8. That is, John the Baptist is Elijah reborn, as Malachi 4:5 says Elijah had to be in the day of the Messiah, and as Jesus confirms (Matthew 11:14). When John the Baptist himself is asked if he is Elijah, he says he is not (John 1:21), and if he were the fact would contradict the whole negative attitude to literal-descriptive reincarnation in Chris-

tianity. Great difficulties here for the single vision: none whatever for a metaphorical language in which the paradox of 'is and
is not' is functional.

The question often arises, Why can't we have it both ways?
Why can't there be a definitive literal-descriptive dimension
along with a spiritual vision of it? The reason, apart from the
contradictions and inconsistencies involved, is that the former is
a passive response and the latter an active one, and if they were
both there the passive one would take over and eliminate the
active one. The human mind, like the human body, has a
strong pull toward inertia built into it. Most religions teach a
doctrine of immortality that by definition implies a release of a
new source of unfettered energy at death, but the great majority
of petitions for the after-death state ask for peace, repose,
untroubled sleep in the bosom of God. 'After the first death,
there is no other,' says Dylan Thomas, saying something that
those who accept immortality and those who do not can agree
on.

Similarly, faith involves risk and adventure: it cannot rest in
assured certainties, because there are no certain propositions that
are not tautologies. Two and two certainly make four, but only
because four is another way of saying two and two. The practical
certainties of sense experience, or the self-assurance that one
would have had them at the time specified, neutralize the
genuine energy of faith. Hence Sir Thomas Browne's remark in
Religio Medici: 'I bless myself and am thankful ... that I never saw
Christ nor his disciples.' A Chinese philosopher is said to have
remarked that in practice unicorns do not exist, because if
anyone saw a unicorn he would instantly tell himself that he
had not seen it and forget the memory. The spirit of this remark
is in the Gospels too, where so frequently people do not hear
what they hear, and do not see what they see. The 'both ways'
we have, therefore, are only the alternatives of the choice
between using the Gospels as spiritual batteries, so to speak, for
charging one's spiritual energies, and looking at them objectively
as aesthetic productions.

In pagan religion two factors stand out: the personal focus, associated with the temporal ruler, and the sense of nature as a manifestation of law, which accompanied the decline of belief in the earlier capricious gods. I will look at the personal focus first. One who voluntarily assumes responsibility and devotes himself to decision and action enters a situation of guilt, however admirable his motives in doing so may be. Lying, half-truths, the threat of violence, pressures of self-interest, surround him on all sides, and it takes exceptional integrity, astuteness, and a certain amount of luck to avoid being infected by them. Even the idealized description of the magnanimous man in Aristotle's *Nicomachean Ethics* gives the impression of a kind of moral ballet dancer, whose skill in avoiding error attracts more admiration than his actual virtue. To acquire power, on the other hand, is to be led into temptation, from which the Lord's Prayer asks deliverance, and the temporal ruler, for all the adulation he may receive in his lifetime, seldom lasts long as a role model.

The spiritual personality of Jesus as set out in the Gospels, however, remains unchanged as a role model, or rather as *the* role model, for Christians. He remains aloof from decision and action, apart from those decisions that affect his own life, but is totally concerned with the world, even though he has a high regard for privacy. What he does is renounce temporal power, as the episode of his arrest shows in particular. Anyone with his abilities of concentration might have been able to eliminate much of the physical pain of the Crucifixion, but it seems clear that he was called upon to renounce that too. It is only after his resurrection that he says, 'All power is given unto me.' Yet there is nothing ghostly about him, and nothing of the sense of antagonism between soul and body. In fact he is ridiculed as one who 'comes eating and drinking' (Luke 7:34) instead of being, like Plotinus, an ascetic ashamed of being in a body, as holy men are often conventionally supposed to be.

The ideal portrayed here has parallels in other religions: one is the hero of the *Tao te ching* in China who seeks the humble 'way of the valley' and the kind of non-action out of which all effective action ultimately comes. But this remains on the level of precept only, and even so the supreme sacrifice of dying for the people does not appear to be anything that would appeal to a Taoist. The dilemma faced by pagans in trying to get their gods to behave decently, and thereby including them in a growing sense of order and coherence in both society and nature, is much more complex. For the Epicureans, including Lucretius, the gods can preserve their integrity only by not soiling their hands with human affairs. Stoics and Neoplatonists took less easy ways out; but here Christianity itself had a crucial problem. We said that the sole basis of the revelation of the Messiah in the New Testament is the Old Testament; but what does the Old Testament provide us with?

The Humanized God

The Jehovah of the Old Testament develops into a monotheistic God out of the stage known as henotheism, where he is specifically the God of Israel, without the reality of heathen and hostile gods being denied. Syrian invaders explain to each other (I Kings 20:24) that Jehovah is the god of a hilly country, skilful therefore at hill-fighting, so that the Israelites have to be enticed to lower ground in order to make him ineffective. We are here on the Homeric level of gods fighting each other, when Trojan gods are defeated along with the Trojans. Of course this is only a heathen army getting it wrong, but we also read of 'contests' with Dagon of Philistia and Baal of Phoenicia. And while many aspects of Jehovah rank with the highest possible conceptions of God, such as the shepherd of the Twenty-third Psalm and the suffering servant of the second Isaiah, the God of the Old Testament is on the whole not presented as a theologian's model or perfect being, but as an intensely humanized figure, as violent and unpredictable as King Lear.

What, for example, are we to do with a God who drowns the world in a fit of anger and repeoples it in a fit of remorse, promising never to do it again (Genesis 9:11); a God who curses the ground Adam is forced to cultivate after his fall, but removes the curse after Noah makes a tremendous holocaust of animals, the smell of their burning flesh being grateful to his nose (Genesis 8:21); a God who rejects Saul as king after he spares his enemy Agag out of human decency (because he should have been offered to God as a sacrifice) and inspires Samuel to hew Agag in pieces and tell Saul that he has committed an unforgivable sin (I Samuel 15); a God who observes children mocking the prophet Elisha and sends bears out to eat up the children (II Kings 2:23), and so on? All mythologies have a trickster God, and Jehovah's treatment of the Exodus Pharaoh (hardening his heart), of Abraham, perhaps even of Job, shows clear trickster affinities. Some of the most horrendous of his capers, such as the sacrifice of Isaac, are tests or trials of faith, implying a lack of knowledge of what is already in Abraham's mind and will. We spoke of the pagan gods who reflected the whimsical and capricious elements in a still unknown and mysterious nature; but is there any real superiority to that stage here?

We notice first the stark simplicity of the biblical scenario, in contrast to the complexities both of polytheism and of later theologies. There are only God and Israel, though Israel may be in different contexts an individual, a society, or a metonymy for the human race. Jesus himself is a spiritual Israel in individual form. Again, Jehovah has nothing of the 'Olympian' about him, nothing of the god who is removed from the human situation unless something exceptional attracts his attention: his preoccupation with his people is continuous, insistent to the verge of fussiness.

When we look at the Bible from the point of view of later Christianity, we often get a vision of a God sitting up in a metaphorical sky, presiding over moral and natural law, omnipotent, omniscient, loving, compassionate, merciful – all the right words – but leaving the outcries of pain and misery from the world below largely unheeded. To his devotees he is the source of grace, a quality or power almost always associated with metaphors of descending from a remote height. To others he seems a picture of impotence, an empty hypothesis.

This is not intended to be anything but a caricature: what I am describing is the disparity between this metaphorical structure and the intensely limited and concrete relation of God and man to which the Bible mainly confines itself. This is especially true of the Mosaic books, which set out God's intimate, even cosy, relations with Adam, Noah, Abraham, Jacob, and Moses. To the writing prophets God is still close, but mainly as an invisible voice. Yet even in the wisdom literature, while terms of infinite transcendence are certainly applied to God, there is little interest in God's traditional metaphysical attributes. With Jesus' relation to his Father in the Gospels, the original intimacy is not only restored but increased to the point of identity ('I and my Father are one'). Nowhere does the Bible seem to be afraid of the word anthropomorphic.

We often meet with miraculous events in the Bible, such as the triumphant vindication of Elijah on Mount Carmel before the priests of Baal (I Kings 18), where a voice within us keeps insisting that God does not act in this way, that he does not interrupt the course of nature arbitrarily, and that a contemporary of ours who attempted Elijah's feat would encounter the same silence that the priests of Baal did. To cling to the authenticity of the event sooner or later suggests the question, If God could do it then, why can't he do it now? This is the attitude of looking for a 'sign' that Jesus condemns (Matthew 12:39). In any case the historical event, whatever it was, is out of our range: it is only the verbal event that concerns us, and the verbal event may be the starting-point of an adventure in understanding. This story in particular illustrates the curious intimacy of God and man which seems uniquely biblical. Magicians and miracle-workers are worldwide, but only in the Bible would God and his prophet cooperate in putting on a show for a public. And however 'incredible' we may find the story, its haunting power has some connection with all the occasions where the wrong kind of help has let us down and only the authentic kind breaks through.

At this point we are still on the metaphorical-literal level where stories are simply stories, considered with the suspended judgment of the imagination without relation to the area we vaguely describe as 'truth.' Beyond that lie the 'polysemous' levels in which the biblical stories form a myth to live by, transformed from the kind of story we can construct ourselves to a spiritual story of what has created and continues to re-create us. According to Milton, the Bible should be read by the 'rule of charity.' That is, the Bible is the charter of human freedom, and any approach to it that rationalizes the enslaving of man has something wrong with it. For example, when chloroform was discovered and doctors began to use anaesthetics to lessen the pain of childbirth, some clergymen objected that this violated the commandment in Genesis 3:16: 'In pain shall you bring forth children.' One can read any book as a mirror of oneself, and here, perhaps, we think of the comment of the eighteenth-century writer Lichtenberg that if a monkey looks into a mirror, an angel will not look out. But we should not dismiss such objections as mere perversity, but consider them as examples of the fallacy of a kind of legalism inherent in the literal-descriptive view, according to which every event or prophecy or commandment in the Bible establishes an identical precedent for the present day. One hears this doctrine of precedent often enough from pulpits still, but the application of it in detail would often lead to such absurdities as the example just given.

The next step up from the metaphorical-literal in reading the Bible is traditionally the allegorical, where the story 'really means' something expressible in discursive language. Non-biblical religions allegorized their myths extensively in the effort to give them profounder meanings, and Plato ridicules this procedure (technically called *hyponoia*), as his aim was to supplant mythology with dialectic. The biblical religions had to go in the direction of *hyponoia*, however, as they had only their stories. But the discursive element in allegory keeps something of the divisive 'I must be right and you must be wrong' quality in it.

Paul, for example, refers to the story in Genesis of Abraham's two wives, in which one wife became jealous of the other and succeeded in getting her rival sent into the desert. Paul says that this story is an 'allegory' (Galatians 4:24) in which the excluded wife represents the bondage of the Jewish law and the accepted one the freedom of the Christian gospel. A Jewish reader of Paul's interpretation, seeing that the Jews are identified with the Ishmaelites and the Christians with the Jews, might well say that this view of the story was about the most preposterous that it was possible to hold, and that a method of this kind could say anything about anything. A further advance in meaning is clearly needed, something that goes in a more catholic direction, such as 'Freedom is within the orbit of God's will and bondage is outside it.' Not that Paul would rule out further advances of this sort by any means.

Above the allegorical level, in the medieval system, is the moral or tropological level, the reading of the Bible that takes us past the story into the reordering and redirecting of one's life. The clearest examples of this kind of meaning are probably the parables of Jesus, explicitly fictions, but fictions that end with 'Go, and do thou likewise.' The divisiveness we noted at the allegorical level remains to some degree in all religions, in the form of 'This makes sense to me if not to you,' but it is difficult to argue against the human compassion in such stories as those of the good Samaritan and the prodigal son. We may note that the former story ascribes a genuine charity to someone outside both the Jewish and the embryonic Christian communions. With such parables we begin to suspect that there may be two readers within us, and that one is beginning to form a larger vision that the other has only to attach itself to. That is, we are moving from a single or natural vision to a double or spiritual one.

This movement is a purgatorial journey in which God and man are visualized as working within the same human units, whether individual or social. A glance at the human situation around us reveals war, famine, arbitrary acts of injustice and exploitation, violence, crime, collapse of moral standards, and so on almost indefinitely. Even in prosperous countries a spiritual barrenness produces innumerable acts of ferocity and despair. How does human life of this kind differ from life in hell? Hell is often supposed to be an after-death state created by God in which people are eternally tortured for finite offences. But this doctrine is merely one more example of the depravity of the human mind that thought it up. Man alone is responsible for hell, and much as he would like to pursue his cruelties beyond the grave, he is blocked from doing so. God's interest in this hell is confined to 'harrowing' or redeeming those who are in it. At the same time there are honesty, love, neighbourliness, generosity, and the creative powers in the arts and sciences. Human life appears to be a mingling of two ultimate realities, which we call heaven and hell. Hell is the world created by man, and heaven, or at least the way to it, is the world created through man by God.

Hence the stories of the Bible may exhibit all three of the levels we spoke of in connection with Milton's *Paradise Regained*: demonic parody, redemptive power, and apocalyptic vision. The name Israel, which is traditionally supposed to mean 'one who strives with God,' was given to Jacob after the extraordinary episode in Genesis 32 usually called 'wrestling with the angel.' There are some very archaic elements in this story: the 'angel' is, like the demons of darkness, including Hamlet's father, a being who is compelled to disappear at daybreak. He seems also to be a local demon, like the river-god whom Achilles fights with in *Iliad* 21, and who would have destroyed the great hero if the latter had not been given an abundance of supernatural help. The river in Genesis has shrunk to a brook (Jabbok), but traces of a guardian spirit in nature are still there. The Homeric god, though he has a name, is usually referred to by Homer simply as 'river' (*potamos*). Similarly when Jacob asks for the name of his antagonist, he gets no response: he would acquire too much power over his opponent if he knew his name. Another very primitive element is the use of a myth as an explanation of a dietary taboo (v 32).

However anxious the angel is to get away, Jacob clings to him demanding a blessing, though what he eventually gets is a touch in the thigh that lames him for life. The antagonist himself is called a 'man' in verse 24, but he is clearly no man, and by verse 30 we have a very strong hint that in some way and some sense Jacob has been striving with God himself, though surely one can strive with God only by striving with or through oneself to obtain a spiritual vision of God. So we have, first, a demon of darkness who attacks and mutilates those who encounter him, then a redemptive context in which Jacob demands a blessing from an angel, and a final outcome in which Jacob is transformed by divine power into Israel, the individual centre and starting-point of God's people.

The story of the sacrifice of Isaac also has a demonic basis: the sacrifice of human children which was practised around Israel but forbidden to the Israelites themselves. This story also sets up a demonic situation and then moves in a redemptive direction, where Abraham becomes aware of the uncompromising priority of God's right to human devotion against the closest of earthly ties. We may compare Jesus' remark in the Gospels that he had come to bring not peace but a sword, and cause division even among families. The redemptive vision of Abraham is eloquently expounded in Kierkegaard's *Fear and Trembling*, where Kierkegaard's personal sacrifice of his love Regina is part of the situation. There is also a poem by Emily Dickinson where that poet's troubled but utterly honest vision sees the story as a contemptible act of arbitrary tyranny on God's part. Textually speaking, both perspectives are 'true,' but the Dickinson poem remains on the metaphorical-literal level of the story while Kierkegaard explores the redemptive dimension in it.

Sometimes the journey of understanding leads, in Hegelian fashion, to the opposite of what the physical event suggests. Let us imagine a speaker in Flanders or Leningrad or anywhere where there is a war cemetery memorializing hundreds of thousands of dead soldiers, explaining to an audience that aggressiveness is essential to humanity because of its survival value. A kernel of truth in a bushel of vicious nonsense; but in contemplating the nonsense our understanding begins to turn inside out. The conventions of secular literature, as they descend from Homer to medieval romance, keep the aggressive hero in the foreground as a central poetic theme. These conventions are also reflected in the Old Testament period between Joshua and David. Other elements in the Bible eventually push us in the opposite direction of seeing that endurance under adversity is the real form of courage. Here the genuine survival values become the spiritual ones given by faith and hope, even when we are not quite sure what our faith is in or what our hope is for; even when their goal is certain death.

Faith and hope, however, seem to get implicated in the question of the postponed promise. If God promises prosperity to Israel, why so long a period of exile, servitude, even massacres to a point at which only a 'saving remnant' survives? More bluntly, why is God portrayed as incessantly promising better things, when history records so little in the way of performance? Taking Israel to be typical of the human situation as a whole, the question expands into the stock question of what is called theodicy, or why a good God permits evil and suffering.

The virtues of faith and hope are purgatorial virtues, and culminate in the paradisal vision of love. Love in the New Testament is agape or caritas, God's love for humanity reflected in the human love for God and for one's neighbour. The sexual basis of love is subordinated, because the primary emphasis is on the individual and the community, but erotic love is clearly a part of the total vision. Such love, it seems to me, has to begin with the human recognition that it is only human beings who have put evil and suffering into human life, and that no other entity than ourselves, certainly not God, is responsible for its persistence. I have expressed this elsewhere by suggesting that love or charity begins by asking the question, 'Why do we permit so much evil and suffering?' The story of the Exodus shows God in the role of guide to a promised land out of Egypt, the symbolic 'furnace of iron' or hell-world of bondage. He is unalterably opposed to any turning back to this 'Egypt,' and those who try to do so have to face his 'wrath.' But if our general thesis is right, this wrath has nothing of the human egocentric feelings of anger or desire for revenge or love of punishment, however much the rhetoric of the prophets may suggest such things. Wrath is, so to speak, honest criticism, and points out consequences: it does not interfere with free will.

There is certainly a demonic state of being, but it appears to be really an intensification of the human one. Conceivably the divine state is too, or, at least, progress in human love might be thought to bring us to the point of identity with God. Traditional Christianity tends rather to follow the view, which goes back to Augustine at least, that the advance of the spirit, wherever it ends, certainly makes us more authentically human. This is usually taken to refer only to the individual human, but the question arises whether there could be social spiritual advance as well. If so, we are involved again in some conception of progress, though of a very different kind from those mentioned earlier.

Every one of us is defined by our social conditioning, but while our conditioning defines us, it also limits, even imprisons, us, and awareness of the limitations built into being who and what we are is one of the central elements in education, particularly religious education. One of the most encouraging signs of social change in the last half-century is the growing momentum of such awareness, a momentum that has increased to the point of being a social movement. Earlier in the century we realized how much we owed to Marxism for illuminating the 'bourgeois' conditioning of which most of that class had up till then been unconscious. Similar is the Freudian illumination of unconscious conflict in our minds and the way we rationalize it. Both these movements, however, especially Marxism, tended to polarize every situation dialectically, and we are beginning to find this incessant polarizing less and less convincing.

The news media now devote a great deal, perhaps even most, of their attention to the way that our conditioned attitudes block our own freedom, ranging from the cruder stereotypes of racism and sexism to the subtler arrogance in regard to the natural environment. Such a growing awareness also prevents us from a facile idealizing of the past. Bernard of Clairvaux was one of the greatest saints of his time, but by the standards of contemporary awareness anyone who put so much time and energy into preaching a crusade would not be a saint at all, however intense his spiritual life and however numerous his miracles. There may be just wars, but no holy wars, because the 'good' side is never holy and the 'bad' side is still human. The question that concerns us at present is, Can a growing insight into our own conditioned limits also be connected with a process of, so to speak, cleaning up the human picture of God?

Such a phrase as 'consciousness-raising' may often refer to

niggling pedantries of no real importance; but behind it is something that could be of revolutionary religious significance. The single vision of God sees in him the reflection of human panic and rage, its love of cruelty and domination, and, when it accepts such a God, calls on him to justify the maintaining of these things in human life. The double vision sees this as taking the face of God in vain, as it were, and tries to separate the human mirror from God's reality. The point is that his reality comes far closer to human life when purified of the reflection of human evil: that is why the Bible presents so anthropomorphic a picture of him, even in the centuries before the Incarnation.

We must now very briefly sum up the relation of our 'double vision' in language, space, and time to our double vision of God.

One of the benefits of the coming of the kingdom of the spirit, the prophets tell us, is the restoring of a 'pure speech' (Zephaniah 3:9). Such purity can hardly be the abstract purity of logic or descriptive accuracy, much less the isolation of one existing language from others. It is rather the purity of simple speech, the parable or aphorism that begins to speak only after we have heard it and feel that we have exhausted its explicit meaning. From that explicit meaning it begins to ripple out into the remotest mysteries of what it expresses and clarifies but does not 'say.' Not all pure speech is in the Bible: T.S. Eliot and Mallarmé tell us that purifying the speech of the 'tribe' or society around us is what gives a social function to the poet. Such purity of speech is not simply a creative element in the mind, but a power that re-creates the mind, or perhaps has actually created the mind in the first place, as though it were an autonomous force deriving from an authentic creation; as though there really were a Logos uniting mind and nature that really does mean 'Word.'

We also spoke of Blake's double vision, which seems at first to be reverting from the conscious awareness of an objective order to the old superstitious notion of presences haunting it. But we also suggested that Blake is really talking about a third stage of development, one in which the vision of gods comes back in the form of a sense of identity with nature, where nature is not merely to be studied and lived in but loved and cherished, where place becomes home. A new covenant with nature, Hosea tells us (2:18), will come after war has been swept from the face of the earth. The growth of nature from a manifestation of order and intellectual coherence into an object of love would bring about the harmony of spirit and nature that has been a central theme of this work. Some recent writers have been deeply impressed by the conception in Chinese culture of a harmony between two similar worlds, usually translated as 'heaven' and 'earth,' which is the goal of all genuinely human aspiration. We should perhaps not overlook the fact that what seems like the same kind of harmony is prominently featured in the Lord's Prayer.

Our physical bodies are part of a world usually described as material, but if matter is simply energy cooled down to the point at which our physical bodies can live with it, perhaps spirit can enter a world of higher energies where the separate things spread around objective heres and theres are no longer things to keep bumping into. In such a spiritual nature, a nature of 'implicate order,' as it has been called, or interpenetrating energies, and no longer the nature of congealed objects, we should be gods or numinous presences ourselves. If the spirit of man and the spirit of God inhabit the same world, that fact is more important than the theological relation between them.

Reverting to our remark about the God of promises, all our conditioning is rooted in our temporal existence and in the anxiety that appears in the present as the passing of time and in the future as death. If death is the last enemy to be destroyed, as Paul tells us, the last metaphor to be transcended is that of the future tense, or God in the form of Beckett's Godot, who never comes but will maybe come tomorrow. The omnipresence of time gives some strange distortions to our double vision. We are born on a certain date, live a continuous identity until death on another date; then we move into an 'after'-life or 'next' world where something like an ego survives indefinitely in something like a time and place. But we are not continuous identities; we have had many identities, as babies, as boys and girls, and so on through life, and when we pass through or 'outgrow' these identities they return to their source. Assuming, that is, some law of conservation in the spiritual as well as the physical world exists. There is nothing so unique about death as such, where we may be too distracted by illness or sunk in senility to have much identity at all. In the double vision of a spiritual and a physical world simultaneously present, every moment we have lived through we have also died out of into another order. Our life in the resurrection, then, is already here, and waiting to be recognized.

Notes

p 3, line 19. The United Church of Canada was formed in 1925 by union of the Presbyterian, Methodist, and Congregational churches of Canada. It is Canada's largest Protestant church.

p 13, line 11. 'one writer.' Richard Dawkins, *The Selfish Gene* (1976)

p 17, line 18. 'Wallace Stevens.' 'Theory,' in *Collected Poems* (1954), 86.

p 18, line 25. 'Coleridge.' See particularly I.A. Richards, *Coleridge on Imagination* (reprinted 1960 with comments by Kathleen Coburn), 98.

p 30, line 34. 'Man's consciousness.' The English language, in its illogical unwisdom, established the convention many centuries ago that 'man' means 'men and women' and 'mankind' humanity. Other languages preserve the same conventions. In my view it is better to let such vestigial constructions fossilize rather than to attempt the pedantries of a uniform 'common language.' The fossilizing process does take place: we no longer think of a 'Quaker' as a hysteric or of 'Christmas' as a mass. Again, it is a distrust of metaphorical thinking that is involved. A seldom noticed aspect of this question is the language of pietistic hymns, one of which begins: 'Safe in the arms of Jesus, / Safe on his gentle breast.' The essential religious feeling here is that the risen Christ, at least, is quite as female as male.

p 32, line 20. 'Kant.' *Critique of Judgment*, tr. J.H. Bernard (1966), section 58

p 33, line 3. The Blake quotation is from *The French Revolution*; the Wallace Stevens one from 'So-and-So Reclining on Her Couch.' *Collected Poems*, 296.

p 36, line 12. 'Hegel.' See *Phenomenology of Spirit*, by G.W.F. Hegel, tr. A.V. Miller with analysis of the text and foreword by J.N. Findlay (1977), section 177. For the 'substance is subject' above see section 18, and for the 'unhappy consciousness' earlier, section 206.

p 39, line 7. 'Caligula.' See Josephus, *Antiquities of the Jews*, XVIII, viii.

p 39, line 15. I am aware that this distinction between 'create' and 'make' does not exist in ordinary language, but the distinction is quite as important as though it did.

p 44, line 27. 'Malekula.' J. Layard's account of Malekulan mythology is well summarized in G.R. Levy, *The Gate of Horn* (1948), 152 ff.

p 45, line 9. 'Anaximander.' See *The Presocratics*, ed. Philip Wheelwright (1966), 53.

p 50, line 15. 'primitive view of history.' Mircea Eliade, *The Sacred and the Profane* (1959), 68 ff

p 50, line 20. 'Pharaoh.' Henri Frankfort, *Ancient Egyptian Religion* (1961), 102 ff

p 57, line 35. 'Coleridge.' *Conciones ad Populum*: 'On the Present War'

p 69, line 29. 'Pietro.' William Anderson, *Dante the Maker* (1980), 347

p 72, line 16. 'Dylan Thomas.' 'A Refusal to Mourn the Death,' etc.

p 73, line 31. 'Plotinus.' The life of Plotinus by his disciple Porphyry begins with the statement that Plotinus was ashamed of being in the body.

p 77, line 2. 'rule of charity.' Milton, *De Doctrina Christiana*

p 80, line 14. 'Emily Dickinson.' *Collected Poems*, ed. Thomas H. Johnson, 1317

p 83, line 23. The line 'to purify the dialect of the tribe,' in Eliot's 'Little Gidding' is derived from Mallarmé's 'Le tombeau d'Edgar Poe.'

p 84, line 20. 'implicate order.' David Bohm, *Wholeness and the Implicate Order* (1980), ch. 7